2.734
off
7 oo
/14

Praise for *Praying Through Your Adoption*:

Adoption is all about love. Michele Scott candidly tells us about their love amidst the real life challenges of adoption. She teaches us how to pray with Scripture, giving us hope and strength. I recommend this book to all families involved in the adoption process.

—**William J. Blacquiere**
President/CEO of Bethany Christian Services

Praying Through Your Adoption is a powerful reminder that throughout the adoption process, you are not alone. The narrative provides a community of parents who share their joys, disappointments, and fears, but ultimately celebrate the story of how the Lord provided for them throughout the adoption process. It is an encouragement for anyone embarking on the journey of adoption—I just wish my wife Laurel and I had had this resource when we adopted our son!

—**Peter Greer**
President of HOPE International and
co-author of *The Poor Will Be Glad*

To "defend the fatherless" and "set the lonely in families" through adoption and foster care is to mirror God's heart. It is a sacred commitment, and a matter with spiritual dimensions that exceed our ability to comprehend. It will almost certainly carry both great difficulty and great joy. So we would do well to approach this journey like Moses at the burning bush--with reverence, humility, supplication, and thanksgiving. Prayer is the wellspring of all of this, and *Praying Through Your Adoption* provides invaluable help for learning in practical terms how to walk this unparalleled journey with God.

—**Jedd Medefind**
President of Christian Alliance for Orphans

Adoption can be a scary experience. It's often very unfamiliar and quite unpredictable, and the stakes are high. King Jesus has given us one place to run in times of anxiety: the cry to the Father in prayer. This book will equip adopting families and their friends with exactly what we need: practical tools for praying through the process of adoption or foster care, from beginning to end. Read it, and pray.

—**Russell D. Moore**
Author of *Adopted for Life: The Priority of Adoption for Christian Families and Churches*

Praying Through Your Adoption is rich with resources you won't find anyplace else. As an adoptive mother and a person of faith, I would have loved to have had this book when walking through the adoption of my son seven years ago! As someone who was adopted in infancy, I thank the Lord this is now available to the parents being used to love the precious children so dear in God's heart.

—**Margot Starbuck**
Author of *The Girl in the Orange Dress: Searching for a Father Who Does Not Fail*

As a pastor, I recognize the need to provide families for orphans through adoption, as many people at Hopewell can attest to. Michele's book is timely, as she has walked this road herself.

—**John Szymanski**
Lead Pastor of Hopewell Christian Fellowship
Elverson, Pennsylvania

Praying Through Your Adoption

Blessings!
Michele Court
Rom 12:12

Praying Through Your Adoption

A Complete Guide to Creating and Nurturing

Today's Forever Family

Michele Cervone Scott

WinePressPublishing
Great Books, Defined.

WinePress Publishing (PO Box 428, Enumclaw, WA 98022) functions only as book publisher. As such, the ultimate design, content, editorial accuracy, and views expressed or implied in this work are those of the author.

Unless otherwise noted, all Scriptures are taken from *The Amplified Bible, Old Testament*, © 1965 and 1987 by The Zondervan Corporation, and from *The Amplified New Testament*, © 1954, 1958, 1987 by The Lockman Foundation. Used by permission.

Scripture references marked NLT are taken from the *Holy Bible, New Living Translation*, copyright © 1996, 2004 by Tyndale Charitable Trust. Used by permission of Tyndale House Publishers, Wheaton, Illinois 60189. All rights reserved.

Scripture references marked NKJV are taken from the *New King James Version*, © 1979, 1980, 1982 by Thomas Nelson, Inc., Publishers. Used by permission.

Scripture references marked MSG are taken from *The Message Bible* © 1993 by Eugene N. Peterson, NavPress, PO Box 35001, Colorado Springs, CO 80935, 4th printing in USA 1994. Published in association with the literary agency—Alive Comm. PO Box 49068, Colorado Springs, CO 80949. Used by permission.

ISBN 13: 978-1-60615-083-2
ISBN 10: 1-60615-083-9
Library of Congress Catalog Card Number: 2010937538

Contents

    A Forever Family
    Parenting After Infertility
    Adopting Domestically
    Adopting Internationally

    Shock and Awe
    From Dream to Reality

    Bathing Your Future Child in Prayer
    Praying for Birth Parents
    Praying for Others Involved in Adoption
    Praying Against Spiritual Warfare

Acknowledgments

T O ERIC, MY husband and complement, for loving me and supporting my dreams.

To Noah, our silly, sweet, and bright bud. I love being your mommy.

To Michael and Betty Cervone and Richard and Jean Scott, we couldn't ask for better parents and grandparents. There aren't enough words to thank you.

To Amy Somerfield, for walking by my side through each of the joys and challenges of this journey.

To Jennifer Brown, Donya Coke, and Judy Willis, my girlfriends and cheerleaders.

To Faye Baylis, neighbor turned assistant and friend, for your many hours spent on this project.

To Eric and Tina Cressman, friends and family photographers, for capturing the heart of our family that day.

To our social worker, Christyn Dodla, and Bethany Christian Services, for riding out the delays and frustrations while facilitating our adoption.

To Tammy Hopf and the wonderful team at WinePress Publishing for a beautiful job!

To Barbara Sher, your inspiration and push made holding this book possible.

To Marlene Bagnull and my writing friends, for advice, critiques, and shared passion.

To all of our friends, neighbors, and service providers too numerous to name, thank you for adding value to our lives and this story.

Most of all, I wish to thank God, Who insists on loving me, saving me, and doing "exceedingly abundantly above all [I could] ask or think" (Ephesians 3:20 NKJV). May this book proclaim that it was He who gave me the gift of a son.

Preface

Pray like crazy.
—Michael Easley on adoption[1]

I HAD ALWAYS hoped to become a mom someday, maybe after focusing on a career. But shortly after marrying my husband, Eric, an unexplained longing surprised me out of nowhere. So when it came time to try to conceive, my Type A personality couldn't resist. I loaded our shelves with books on pregnancy, parenting, and how to pray through every step. Then when we had trouble conceiving, I collected more resources to guide us through the disappointments and decisions.

Our journey to parenthood, as I affectionately call it, soon included adoption. Obviously, I gathered the next round of books, grateful for authors who shared their insights and experiences on this unique calling. But the one resource I could not find is the one you now are holding.

I started writing *Praying Through Your Adoption* during the challenging and dreaded "waiting stage" of adopting our son. Before then, we were guilty of praying for "the adoption" and not necessarily each specific detail. While I believe God's will was accomplished regardless of what we did or did not do, perhaps we missed out on opportunities to partner with Him as He worked.

God's Word provides a constant, unfailing source of love, strength, and comfort. He knows what we're facing and can see us through when others may not understand. Praying with Scripture helps us to draw closer to Him and His power. You can memorize verses, recite them as promises, or rework them as personal, specific prayers. Here is an example:

1. Read, "Wait on the LORD; Be of good courage, And He shall strengthen your heart; Wait, I say, on the LORD!" (Psalm 27:14 NKJV).
2. Pray, "Lord, Your Word says and I believe that as I wait on You and this adoption, You will strengthen my heart" (a promise from Psalm 27:14 NKJV).
3. Pray, "Father God, as we wait on You to be selected by a birth mother, help us be of good courage. Strengthen our hearts against delays and disappointments, knowing You have the right time and the right child in mind for us" (a prayer based on Psalm 27:14 NKJV).

May the prayers, scriptures, and adoption stories in *Praying Through Your Adoption* help guide you as God writes your family's adoption story.

Blessings and prayers,
Michele

Chapter 1

Considering

"Orphans in Africa"[1]

Adoption is a visible gospel. It's really a re-telling of what our story is of coming into God's family.

—Steven Curtis Chapman[2]

A Forever Family

ADOPTION IS A win-win situation: a child needs a family, and a family wants a child. Yet most adoptive families cite challenges, whether in the process of adoption or in parenting their adopted child, when recounting their miraculous stories.

1

How do you know if adoption is right for your family? You don't, really. There are no guarantees in parenting, whether biological or adoptive. Success begins with your willingness to love and impact a child in need, along with your resolve to see it through. Orphans, especially those with difficult starts in life, are resilient survivors. They need parents who will step up to the plate and bat for them with prayer and action.

When I felt God leading us to consider adoption, I jumped in with both feet. Nothing scared me, not the paperwork, interviews, or idea of loving and caring for "someone else's child." The cost seemed prohibitive, but I trusted that the Lord would provide. My husband, Eric, on the other hand, seemed hesitant. In his mind, he couldn't reconcile the idea of parenting without a biological connection.

Barbara Rainey, adoptive mother and wife of FamilyLife's president, Dennis Rainey, believes, "Both of you must know that God is calling you to adoption. It can't just be one of you. It has to be both husband and wife—you have to know together that you are called. You have to have oneness between you that this is what God is calling us to do as a family."[3]

My desire for a child seemed stronger and more vocal than Eric's, yet I needed to yield to Eric's leadership and, ultimately, the Lord. I learned to surrender my will and wait. After hearing dads talk about their children on a church men's retreat, Eric came home and said, "I want to be a dad. It doesn't matter how." With a green light, we started the process to adopt a child from Russia, a country I came to love during a short-term missions trip.

Considering

Questions to ask yourself when considering adoption:

1. What age child do we want to adopt—infant, toddler, or an older child?
2. Do we want to do domestic or international adoption? If domestic, do we want to do a private adoption or go through foster care? If international, which country?
3. Do we go through an agency, an attorney, or adopt independently?
4. Do we want an open or closed adoption? (The type of adoption you choose may determine this for you.)
5. Do we want to adopt a child of a similar or different race?
6. Do we want to adopt a child with minimal or special needs?

In like manner, you married women, be submissive to your own husbands [subordinate yourselves as being secondary to and dependent on them, and adapt yourselves to them], so that even if any do not obey the Word [of God], they may be won over not by discussion but by the [godly] lives of their wives, when they observe the pure and modest way in which you conduct yourselves, together with your reverence [for your husband; you are to feel for him all that reverence includes: to respect, defer to, revere him—to honor, esteem, appreciate, prize, and, in the human sense, to adore him, that is, to admire, praise, be devoted to, deeply love, and enjoy your husband].

—1 Peter 3:1–2

Therefore a man shall leave his father and his mother and shall become united and cleave to his wife, and they shall become one flesh.

—Genesis 2:24

But Ruth said, "Don't force me to leave you; don't make me go home. Where you go, I go; and where you live, I'll live. Your people are my people, your God is my god; where you die, I'll die, and that's where I'll be buried, so help me GOD—not even death itself is going to come between us!"

—Ruth 1:16-17 MSG

This is how Jesus the Messiah was born. His mother, Mary, was engaged to be married to Joseph. But before the marriage took place, while she was still a virgin, she became pregnant through the power of the Holy Spirit.

—Matthew 1:18 NLT

The Spirit Himself [thus] testifies together with our own spirit, [assuring us] that we are children of God. And if we are [His] children, then we are [His] heirs also: heirs of God and fellow heirs with Christ [sharing His inheritance with Him]; only we must share His suffering if we are to share His glory.

—Romans 8:16–17

In this way we are like the various parts of a human body. Each part gets its meaning from the body as a whole, not the other way around. The body we're talking about is Christ's body of chosen people. Each of us finds our meaning and function as a part of his body. But as a chopped-off finger or cut-off toe we wouldn't amount to much, would we? So since we find ourselves fashioned into all these excellently formed and marvelously functioning parts in Christ's body, let's just go ahead and be what we were made to be, without enviously or pridefully comparing ourselves with each other, or trying to be something we aren't.

—Romans 12:4–6 MSG

One Family's Story: A Worthy Challenge

[Adoption] is a long, hard road, but what road is easy? If you're on an easy road, you might want to ask yourself why.

—Carlos Whittaker

PRAYER POINTS

Loving Father, so many orphans need families, and it seems right to open our hearts and our home to a child. Please show us if this is Your time and Your will. If so, give us Your strength for the process ahead and Your love to care for a child we did not birth. We look to You for wisdom and direction for our family.

Parenting After Infertility

When Rachel saw that she bore Jacob no children, she envied her sister, and said to Jacob, "Give me children, or else I will die!"

—Genesis 30:1

Infertility attacked every facet of my life—the emotional, the physical, the spiritual, and the financial. It drained me, but it also put a strain on my relationships with my husband, family, and friends. I longed for a child I never had met. When my hope was deferred month after month and year after year, I couldn't see a light at the end of the tunnel. I became so focused on my own desires and pain that it was hard to imagine that the Lord had a good and perfect plan for me.

Social workers and therapists recommend coming to terms with the pain of infertility before adopting. Acknowledge your pain, and bring it to the Lord. Remind

5

yourself of His unfailing love and faithfulness to you. Then rest in His promises as you wait for Him to answer your prayers for a child. Someone once said, "If God waits longer than you wish, it is only to make the blessing all the more precious."[4]

Hope deferred makes the heart sick, but a dream fulfilled is a tree of life.

—Proverbs 13:12 NLT

For the vision is yet for an appointed time and it hastens to the end [fulfillment]; it will not deceive or disappoint. Though it tarry, wait [earnestly] for it, because it will surely come; it will not be behindhand on its appointed day.

—Habakkuk 2:3

He gives the childless woman a family, making her a happy mother. Praise the LORD!

—Psalm 113:9 NLT

Sing, O barren one, you who did not bear; break forth into singing and cry aloud, you who did not travail with child! For the [spiritual] children of the desolate one will be more than the children of the married wife, says the Lord.

—Isaiah 54:1

For this child I prayed, and the LORD has granted me my petition which I asked of Him.

—1 Samuel 1:27 NKJV

And Isaac prayed much to the Lord for his wife [Rebekah] because she was unable to bear children.

—Genesis 25:21

Children are a gift from the LORD; they are a reward from him.

—Psalm 127:3 NLT

God's gifts and God's call are under full warranty—never canceled, never rescinded.

—Romans 11:29 MSG

We are assured and know that [God being a partner in their labor] all things work together and are [fitting into a plan] for good to and for those who love God and are called according to [His] design and purpose.

—Romans 8:28

For I am well assured and indeed know that through your prayers and a bountiful supply of the Spirit of Jesus Christ (the Messiah) this will turn out for my preservation (for the spiritual health and welfare of my own soul) and avail toward the saving work of the Gospel.

—Philippians 1:19

Blessed be the God and Father of our Lord Jesus Christ, the Father of sympathy (pity and mercy) and the God [Who is the Source] of every comfort (consolation and encouragement), Who comforts (consoles and encourages) us in every trouble (calamity and affliction), so that we may also be able to comfort (console and encourage) those who are in any kind of trouble or distress, with the comfort (consolation and encouragement) with which we ourselves are comforted (consoled and encouraged) by God.

—2 Corinthians 1:3–4

One Family's Story: Hope Deferred

We struggled with infertility for several years before we had a successful pregnancy. But after more treatments without success, we completed the meetings, home study, and mound of paperwork to adopt our second child.

One year passed, then two. Approaching our third year, several leads resulted in more pain and heartbreak. How could I send my daughter to kindergarten with empty arms at home?

Three days after our daughter started kindergarten, we received exciting news: a birth couple had selected our profile! Independently of each other, the birth mother and birth father thought that our daughter was cute, and they really liked our family. Both of their mothers supported their decision. We decided to parent the child. But on the day of the meeting, the birth parents called off both the meeting and the adoption.

Several weeks later, we saw our daughter's bus driver holding a baby at the local fair. They were foster parents with our agency, so we knew that the baby might become available for adoption.

Soon our agency called about a birth mother who wanted to meet with us to adopt the same baby we had seen the bus driver holding. The hospital nurses called her Hope, like the verse on our adoption profile, Jeremiah 29:11, which read "plans to give you hope…"

Hope arrived in our home in time to bond with her new big sister over Christmas break. But then at a May court date, the birth mother revoked her consent, and the adoption was not finalized. Would the Lord allow Hope to be taken from us? We prayed Philippians 4:7, "And the peace of God, which surpasses all understanding, will guard your hearts and minds through Christ Jesus," as well as, "Be still and know that I am God," from Psalm 46:10. Four days later, I wrote about the peace I felt in my journal. We believed this child was meant for our family and were leaving it in the Lord's hands.

The next week, during my morning devotions, I read Daniel 10:12–13: "Do not fear, Daniel, for from the first day that you set your heart to understand, and to humble yourself before your God, your words were heard; and I have come because of your words. But the prince of the kingdom of Persia withstood me twenty-one days." Daniel fasted and prayed for twenty-one days. As far as we can tell from the biblical account, his difficulties came not because Daniel was not a good person or because his prayer was not right but because of a special attack from Satan. It was twenty-one days from May 9, the first court date, until May 30, the next court date. It gave me chills. We had peace that the Lord would work in our favor, peace that only God could give.

On the morning of the second court hearing, our agency called. The birth mother's rights had been terminated. God is good and faithful.

Seven years have passed; time moves on. I am now wrapped up in the many things motherhood brings—music lessons, vision therapy, volunteering at school. I do not think about our infertility much, but each Mother's Day, I remember the ones who feel pain on that day and offer up a prayer. I know the pain of longing for a child. I also know that my God is faithful.

—Linda Hursh

PRAYER POINTS

Heavenly Father, we believe You have given us a heart's desire to become parents. We are waiting on You and trusting You to fulfill this desire. We pray that our crisis of infertility will draw us closer to You and to each other. Please comfort and strengthen us. Keep the pain of our infertility from hindering us. Help us to live with joy and peace as You intend. It may be difficult, but we praise You now for working all things for our good, even when our situation seems hopeless and disappointing.

Adopting Domestically

Domestic adoption can take many forms. There is open adoption, where the birth parents and adoptive parents make and often maintain contact, or closed adoption, where neither set of parents knows details about the other. A domestic adoption can be completed privately (through an agency or attorney) or through foster care and local government agencies. Here are a few things to consider:

1. What age child do I wish to adopt? In domestic adoption, many ages are available, from newborns to teens.
2. How do I feel about special needs? Children with diagnosed conditions, or even older children with difficult backgrounds, require special care. Be sure you are ready to tackle known and unknown situations.
3. Do I have gender, race, or health preferences? Some of these things can be known and considered. But at times, especially if the child is unborn, these preferences cannot be accommodated so easily.
4. What kind of relationship, if any, do I foresee having with the birth parents? (The answer to this will determine whether open or closed adoption is best.)
5. What are my budget constraints? Adoption can get expensive, but the fees for adopting from foster care are minimal. Adoption grants, loans, employer benefits, and fundraisers may be available and are covered in the next chapter.

Considering

One Family's Story: And Baby Makes Three

Mothers say they forget the pain of childbirth once they lay eyes on their beautiful baby. I learned the same is true for the pain of childlessness when a woman makes you the parents of her baby.

In October of 1996, after resolving ourselves to childlessness, my husband and I formed new life goals, like continuing education and career development. I had called Patti to set up a time to introduce her to a new friend who was interested in deaf ministry. It was in the context of that conversation that we talked about our latest feelings regarding adoption, infertility, and babies. When Patti asked if we ever had considered submitting a resume to Your Loving Choices, a pregnancy resource center, we responded with a "why not" attitude. I'm not sure we realized then that a groundwork of God's incredible glory was about to be revealed.

As we walked the journey of adoption, a recurring theme became "the fingerprints of God." They were everywhere. God's hand, God's signature, God performing only what He can do—bringing the people He needed together to complete His plan.

Our journey began on October 22nd—Bill's (my husband) 41st birthday. I was home for lunch when the phone rang. I wasn't going to pick it up, until I heard Patti's voice on the machine saying, "A twenty-two-year-old birth mother has chosen your resume, and she'd like to meet you." It took a while for her words to sink in, and all I could utter was, "Oh, my goodness. Oh, my goodness!" I soon learned that the baby—a boy—was due in January and that the birth mother wanted us as involved as possible from the moment he was born. What a joy it was to call Bill at work to wish him "happy birthday" and to tell him he was going to be a dad!

11

The next step of our journey brought us to a face-to-face meeting with the birth mother. We were all nervous. But in that small office at Your Loving Choices, God was present. We felt an instant comfort, compassion, and love for each other that transformed an informal meeting into an impromptu pizza party. What was supposed to be a brief encounter extended into a day of talking, sharing, and planning together for the little boy who would soon enter our lives.

The next two months flew by as we busied ourselves with the details of homestudies, attorneys, rearranging our apartment, decorating a Noah's ark nursery, and reading books about adoption and babies. Scattered throughout that time were frequent phone calls back and forth between us and the birth mother. We received regular updates on her health, her cravings for Oreos, and her concern for how we were coming along with the idea of soon becoming parents. I would often find myself in tears as I thought about her concern and about the priceless gift she was about to give us. I often marveled at her maturity and at the love she had for this child as she planned for his future with us.

The day finally came—January 5—a Sunday afternoon. We received the call. "I'm going to the hospital. I think this is going to be it." This would be the second time she had called saying she thought she was in labor, the first being New Year's Eve. We waited anxiously for further news. At 10:00 P.M. she called back. "They're going to keep me in the hospital. If I don't deliver tonight, they will induce labor in the morning. Can you come?"

Of course we could come! We wanted to see our son born, and we wanted to be a support to her. However, the next morning we were met with obstacle after obstacle as we tried to prepare for our departure and for the four-hour drive to the hospital. Our departure was delayed until 2:00 that afternoon. By that time, her water had been broken and contractions were becoming more frequent. She and I talked several times by phone. Her concern continued to be for us. She wanted us to know she understood if we couldn't make it in time.

God continued to remind me of His faithfulness and of His hand on this whole journey. I relinquished to Him my desire to be there for my son's birth and just trusted His plan and His timing. How could I deny His sovereignty and His grace? As I looked outside, it was a gorgeous fifty-five-degree day. One of my biggest fears was that our son would be born during a blizzard and we wouldn't be able to get to the hospital at all. That beautiful, sunshiny day was a gift from God and a reminder that indeed all things are in His control and in His hand.

Andrew Scott was born at 5:37 P.M. We walked into the hospital at 5:45. Within an hour of his birth, we were holding our new son, handed to us by his birth mother.

We later learned from her that the circumstances surrounding her pregnancy and planning this adoption had been an instrument of reconciliation for her family. I could see then why God did not allow us to be present for our son's birth. It was time her family needed to have together, time to rejoice over this new life and to support each other as they not only welcomed him but also said "goodbye" to him.

We had two days to share together in the hospital. Some we spent with the birth mother, her family, and our baby. Much we spent as a new threesome—cuddling, feeding, changing, and at times, weeping for the joy of this new baby.

It didn't take us long to fall in love with our new son. Our days were filled with getting to know Andrew, establishing a routine, walking the floor during fussing times, marveling at his little accomplishments, and introducing him to our family and friends.

When we received news that Andrew's birth father had contacted Patti and wanted to meet us at the hearing that would finalize Andrew's adoption, our new family suddenly felt under threat. Even though he said he only wanted to be present so that we all would know that he wasn't abandoning Andrew, a new fear began to grow in us. "Why had this man shown up now? Did he have a hidden agenda to petition for custody of Andrew?" We read that birth fathers also go through a grieving process when their babies are placed for adoption. We wrestled with the desire to be sensitive enough to allow this man to meet his son and our own need to protect our new family.

The morning of the hearing I was filled with anxious feelings as I rode in the back seat with Andrew. We wanted to have the hearing over with so that Andrew would officially be our son. I couldn't help but worry about whether or not this little car seat would carry our son home with us after the hearing. What if his birth father took him? What if something went wrong? I held that little hand and whispered prayers to God, asking Him to manifest Himself in this last leg of our journey.

Once in the courthouse waiting room, a sudden "family reunion" took place. Andrew's birth mother couldn't wait to see him again. She held him, checked to see if he had big toes like her own, and talked with us about his routines—how he ate and slept. She listened and smiled as we shared with her our love for our son.

Listening from the sidelines was Andrew's birth father. We exchanged hellos and cautious small talk. We then felt compelled to do what some would call risky. We handed our precious little boy to this man and introduced him for the first time to his son.

Soon it was time for the hearings to begin. They were quick, terse, and uneventful. After doing some necessary paperwork in the clerk's office, we returned to the waiting room to find Andrew nestled in the arms of his birth father drinking a bottle. Suddenly, we didn't want to leave. The life and love shared for a little boy had brought us here, and for just a short time, we wanted to share it together. Once again, what was to be a brief, formal encounter, was turning into a morning-long celebration with Andrew at its center.

The threat of a coming storm eventually routed us to go our separate ways. We hugged and thanked Andrew's birth father for sharing this day with us. With sadness in his eyes, he wished us happiness, and he was gone.

Before we left, I looked into the next room to see Andrew and his birth mother sharing a special goodbye. I don't know what she may have said to him, but I have a feeling it may have had to do with God's faithfulness and how she had seen God's hand over us all.

—Melinda Izzo

One Family's Story: Choosing Izaiah

"Please tell the judge why you want to adopt Izaiah," the attorney said.

How could I explain how the baby who had come into my life almost two years ago fit into our family like the last piece of a puzzle? How could I convey how my heart had grown to make room for one more set of first steps, one more first word, and millions more hugs and kisses?

When we started our foster care journey almost four years ago, my husband, Ken, was stumped. He couldn't understand what made me think we needed to have another child. Matthew and Emily were finally at the age where we could take them anywhere, and it was easy. No U-Haul of paraphernalia followed our minivan anymore. We are an on-the-go kind of clan. "We have one of each; they don't make anything else," he would say.

The only way I could put into words the ache in my heart for another child was a visual that had flashed through my head from time to time for over a year. I explained to him that when I looked into the future in my mind, that proverbial "where do you see yourself in five years," our family was sitting on a couch, posing for a photo, and I could see Ken, myself, Matthew, and Emily clearly—but there was one more joining our group. A small child sat on my lap, but I just couldn't see the child's face. I truly believed God was saying, "I have one more."

Many years ago, I was talking to my mom about having more children, and she was thinking I had lost my mind because Matthew and Emily came into the world one right after the other. "Well, how many more?" she asked. I explained that I never would stop at three because that would make Emily the middle child, and she is the more sensitive of the two so it would have to be two more. Four children. "Unless," I clarified, "I could guarantee that third child was a boy. Then she would be the only girl, and maybe that would offset that middle child syndrome." We both agreed that it was not a possibility to guarantee gender. Now I know that we never should say never.

Almost four years ago, when we were starting our journey with the Child Welfare system, my friends would ask me, "How are you going to give the children back?" They knew me, and if you know me, you know that my love for children is embedded in my fingerprints. It is just a huge part of who I am. I had no answer. I didn't want to think about it. I couldn't explain. I, too, couldn't fathom how I would be able to give back the scared and abused children we would love, but I had an unexplainable peace about it, so I just trusted God.

Around this time, I had a dream. You know those dreams that stick with you for days? The ones you just can't shake? That was what this dream was like. There was a baby, a strawberry blond, tiny little boy. The dream lasted only a few scenes before I awoke, but I felt like I knew that baby. For days I would get a jolt only a mother could get, "*Gasp.* Who's got the baby?" It was almost as though I had been given a divine responsibility to that child. Little did I know, I had.

Just the other day as I was looking through an old journal, I came across the entry about that dream. I did the math. I had that dream right around the time Izaiah was conceived. The time was coming.

April 25, 2006, our third child came into our lives as a scared, very tiny, strawberry blond nine-month-old—a child who nervously would visit his birth parents at the courthouse weekly, a child who we were told would go back home soon. Well, because God works miracles, today, April 9, 2008, twenty of his fans (closest family and friends) filed into a courtroom and witnessed Izaiah's adoption finalized. And then there were three.

The past two years of first words, scraped knees, and other childhood milestones were summed up in four words. The judge declared our adoption final, and our five best friends held up an Izaiah-sized t-shirt with the words, "FINALLY A BROWNLOW" printed on the front. Izaiah reached for the shirt and squealed, "ME!"

—Michelle Kemper Brownlow

Prayer Points

Decisions about domestic adoption:

Lord, we have decisions to make about our domestic adoption. Are You calling us to adopt through a birth mother or through foster care? Does Your plan include ministering to a birth mother, and would we consider open adoption (Exodus 2)? Or, should we parent a foster child who is waiting for a family? Should we consider siblings? What about travel outside of our area to complete the adoption?

Father, give us wisdom as we make these decisions. Help us to select the right agency or attorney. Give us Your words and insights to complete the applications, home study interviews, and paperwork with complete honesty. Show us what to include in our family profile. Help us to write a "Dear birth mother" letter that expresses love and compassion for her yet demonstrates our ability to parent.

Adoption from birth parents:

Father, we are now in the process of our domestic adoption. It's exciting to get approved and register our profile. Guard our hearts, especially if we learn we are being considered by birth parents. Prepare us if we meet them. Being chosen could mean an end to our waiting for a child or another disappointment. Help us to remain patient and flexible as You carry us through this process.

May we seek Your best for the child and birth family, placing their needs above our desires. Pour out Your love and blessings upon them. Help us to consider their lives, feelings, and interests apart from us and this *pregnancy. Give them courage and wisdom to make the right decision, and surround them with Your love and a knowledge of Your presence.*

Adoption through foster care:

    Father, we are now in the process of adopting a waiting child. We are excited, and we know You are in control. Keep us patient and flexible as You carry us through the process. Give the social workers wisdom as they evaluate cases for a potential match.

    May we seek Your best for any child proposed to us. Prepare us if we get to meet a child. Make us sensitive to his or her personality, background, and needs. Give us courage and wisdom to make the right decision for us and for the child. We pray now for our future child's birth family and the circumstances that make our child available for us to adopt him or her. Give the birth family wisdom to make good decisions. Surround them with Your love and a knowledge of Your presence.

Adopting Internationally

I believe international adoption, in which we were pioneers, is a true leap of faith. God creates each adoptive family and brings our children home to us across continents and oceans, defying all manner of trials until our children arrive "home" to us.

—Lana Noone[5]

Adopting internationally can be a good closed-adoption option. Depending on the country, eligible children range in age from infant to teen and usually are cared for in orphanages or foster homes. Here are some aspects to consider:

1. What age child do I wish to adopt? In international adoption, newborns are seldom available. Older infants and toddlers through teens are available.
2. How do I feel about special needs? Children with diagnosed conditions, or even older children with difficult backgrounds, require special care, not to mention any culture, language, or post-institutionalized challenges. Be sure you are ready to tackle known and unknown situations.
3. Do I have gender, race, or health preferences? Many of these preferences can be accommodated.
4. How do I feel about international travel and the number of days or trips necessary to complete the adoption? Some countries require one or two trips, while others allow you to send a representative to escort your child home to you. Each country sets its own policies. Check the details specific to the country you are considering.
5. How will my family, friends, and community receive my child? How will I incorporate my child's culture into family life?
6. What are my budget constraints? International adoption gets expensive due to agency, country, and travel fees. Consider financing options, such as adoption grants, loans, employer benefits, and fundraisers (discussed in the next chapter).

One Family's Story: China Doll

The humidity of the bleached, drab room was stifling and thick as London fog. It made breathing difficult, uncomfortable. It was also very warm, even for late May in a foreign land. Like bubbling lava, perspiration puckered from every pore as I raised the camera to my face. It was time.

"Smith family? Smith?" A petite Chinese woman then emerged from a secluded hallway. She was holding a tiny baby girl. The child, one month shy of her first birthday, was bundled up from head to toe in a thick, cotton blanket. I could see only her oval, dark eyes and a tuft of jet black hair. Everything else was concealed. And unlike several of the other babies already presented to other anxious American parents, our little girl did not cry. Initially, in fact, she resembled a cute little doll baby, a porcelain China doll one might find in an upscale antiques gallery.

My wife proudly stepped forward with a smile and accepted the tiny child from the orphanage nanny while I snapped away, trying to eternally capture the moment on film. And just like that, we were parents.

On our honeymoon in Bermuda nine years prior, we had decided to start our family right away. But weeks and months eventually led to years of false pregnancies, miscarriages, failed fertility attempts, medical examinations, wasteful procedures, and profound disappointment. Adoption seemed like our last realistic choice. So, after careful research and prayer, we started the process to adopt from China through Bethany Christian Services.

For fifteen months, we assembled mountain chains of paperwork; visited teams of doctors, case workers, and notaries; counted every penny; pooled financial resources; and diligently prayed. But mostly, we waited... and waited. We sympathized with Tom Petty, who once sang that the hardest part of an experience is the waiting you have to do.

Finally, our caseworker produced a single photo of our future daughter; her chubby cheeks, wispy hair, and vibrant eyes stared into the lens at us. Her name was Ji Hua Chen, but we already knew her as Rebekah Joy Smith, our answer to prayer and personal miracle delivered straight from the hallowed halls of heaven. We sat silently for a few minutes. We had fallen in love.

One month later, we endured a fifteen-hour, 9,000 mile ordeal, involving multiple airports and flights, from America's eastern coast to mainland China. The first night in China went surprisingly smoothly. Rebekah slept most of the time, and we felt this "parenting thing" would be smooth sailing. But by the second day, the wheels came off. Rebekah had a burning fever, wasn't eating well, seemed irritable, and had diarrhea. We sought parental advice from the other families on our trip. They were younger than we were, but we shrugged off any embarrassment in place of help. Tendered mothers and seasoned fathers handed out hugs, remedies, antidotes, prayers, and reassurance.

Changing diapers proved to be the most challenging experience for first time parents in a faraway land. When my wife left for the lobby, in search of cold beverages, I used half a box of wipes and three diapers for my first solo diaper change. Rebekah's diarrhea made it interesting, but somehow we both survived.

After five days, we journeyed home to Delaware, where we were greeted by joyous family members at the final gate. Exhausted but thankful, we embraced each one and passed Rebekah from one set of eager arms to the next.

Few people experience a miracle in their lifetime, but we have been blessed by two. After only five months back on homeland soil, my wife, Geralynn, discovered she was pregnant (a miracle first prophesied by the Bishop of our church several weeks before we traveled to China). We learned firsthand that God does not lie, when nine months later, we held handsome and healthy Matthew Robert Smith in our arms. Now Rebekah had a little brother with whom she could play, grow, and share birthdays, holidays, and Sunday school—and who, on occasion, she could torment.

Children grow up fast, so we've learned to enjoy each moment. In a flash, today becomes yesterday, a memory filed away. The beautiful, Asian infant in swaddling wraps is now a tomboyish fan of Hannah Montana and her mother's Washington Redskins. She rides her Disney princess bicycle, plays soccer, throws pebbles in the ocean, and eats Spaghetti-Os. Soon she'll begin first grade.

My China doll likes to harass her little brother, the four-year-old ball of energy who runs around our noisy, chaotic house these days. And we wouldn't change a thing.

—David Michael Smith

Prayer Points

Decisions about international adoption:

Lord, we have decisions to make regarding international adoption. Should we parent a child from another culture and, if so, from which country? Guide us in requesting an infant or an older child, or even a sibling group. Help us to handle the possibility of knowing very little about our child's background and family health history.

Grant us wisdom to select the right agency, and Your words and insights as we complete applications, home study interviews, and paperwork with complete honesty. Give us and our representatives favor with the officials in the country we have chosen. May we love and respect their country and culture as if it were our own.

In the process of international adoption:

Father, we are now in the process of our international adoption. We are completing paperwork, interviews, and a dossier to be viewed by officials in a foreign country. We are excited, and we know You are in control. Grant us favor with government officials, orphanage directors, and anyone working on behalf of orphans in the country we have chosen. Give them wisdom to make the best decisions, and make us patient and flexible as You carry us through this process.

We pray for our future child's birth family and the circumstances that make our child available for adoption. Surround them with Your love and a knowledge of Your presence.

Prepare us physically and financially to travel internationally or to send a representative to complete the adoption.

Chapter 2

Financing

Once the "what" is decided, the "how" always follows. We must not make the "how" an excuse for not facing and accepting the "what."

—Pearl S. Buck[1]

Shock and Awe

WHEN WE FIRST considered adopting internationally, I gasped at the fees. We didn't have tens of thousands of dollars sitting in a bank account, nor did we want to accumulate debt. Then I recalled how the Lord had provided when I'd left a good-paying job to work for the church, even though it didn't make sense on paper. Subsequently, we determined to step through every open door for whatever funds were necessary to complete our adoption. I decided that if people can spend this kind of money on a vehicle that might only last ten years, it would be much more valuable to spend it on an orphan who needs a family. We reviewed and cut our spending, from telephone and cable bills to requesting a budget plan for our electric service.

From Dream to Reality

At times, we faced unexpected expenses for additional paperwork and fee increases without the help of an adoption grant or employer adoption benefits. But God came through with gifts and loans from family and a last-minute grant and payment plan through our agency (for a fee increase at the end of our adoption). We considered this a confirmation that adoption was His plan for our family.

> Immediately the father of the child cried out and said with tears, "Lord, I believe; help my unbelief!"
> —Mark 9:24 NKJV

> And my God will liberally supply (fill to the full) your every need according to His riches in glory in Christ Jesus.
> —Philippians 4:19

> Unless the LORD builds the house, They labor in vain who build it.
> —Psalm 127:1a NKJV

> No unbelief or distrust made him (Abraham) waver (doubtingly question) concerning the promise of God, but he grew strong and was empowered by faith as he gave praise and glory to God, fully satisfied and assured that God was able and mighty to keep His word and to do what He had promised. That is why his faith was credited to him as righteousness (right standing with God). But [the words], It was credited to him, were written not for his sake alone, but [they were written] for our sakes too. [Righteousness, standing acceptable to God] will be

granted and credited to us also who believe in (trust in, adhere to, and rely on) God, Who raised Jesus our Lord from the dead.

—Romans 4:20–24

One Family's Story: Financial Solutions to the Adoption Option

Over the years, Mark and I occasionally had talked about becoming foster parents. We enjoyed parenting, had a heart for raising children according to God's truths, and always wondered what it might be like to extend that passion beyond our biological family. Even so, we really never had considered adoption.

In January of 2003, a friend casually shared with me a picture of a boy living in an orphanage in Russia. As she handed me the picture, she asked, "Do you know any family who might be interested in adopting a nine-year-old little boy from Russia whose best friend was adopted by a family here in town just eighteen months ago?" I glanced down at the picture and caught my breath. This little guy looked just like my boys. He looked like he belonged in our family. I dismissed the thought immediately, but I couldn't forget that little face.

I found the picture again later that same day. When my husband came home unexpectedly early, I shared the picture and story with him. He became quiet and then said, "This little guy looks like he belongs in our family." At that point, we decided to commit it to prayer.

After just a day, both of us still were very drawn to making this little guy a part of our family. We decided to discuss the possibility with our children, and all four of them responded very positively and with much excitement. We officially decided to pursue making Kolya (pronounced "Cola") a part of our family.

The biggest challenge, however, was the financial piece of this picture. As a limited-income family in full-time ministry, we had worked hard to become debt-free and just had begun to build our savings after several years of struggling financially. So how could we even begin to think about adoption expenses of $25,000–$30,000? That was the most faith-stretching part of the adoption journey, but one where we experienced God's incredible provision and faithfulness.

We found four primary ways to make the adoption option a financial reality. Following is some information on these options.

Creative Fund-raising

As we began to pursue the adoption process, we prayed about and brainstormed fund-raising ideas. Our first venture was a simple woodworking project that the whole family participated in making. We made small cardholders for children to use when playing card games like Uno and Rook. We sold these at a parenting conference and made over $1,000.

Soon after, our eighteen-year-old daughter came up with another fundraiser she called "Cooking For Kolya." After creating an order form listing our family's favorite recipes, she asked teachers, neighbors, family, and friends if they would be interested in ordering anything from an entire meal to a pan of brownies. She raised almost $1,000 and continued to receive orders.

Some families view their adoption as a mission experience and send out support letters to family and friends in order to give them an opportunity to invest in the life of a child. Other families organize community events and other creative fund-raising events to make their dream come true.

Financing

Employer Benefits

Many companies offer adoption benefits to their employees. Some may offer up to $6,000 to adoptive families, and others grant employees parental leave.

Government Assistance

Families now can receive a federal adoption "tax credit" for just over $12,000 for expenses incurred when adopting a child.

Foundations and Ministries

Many organizations exist to encourage and support families in the adoption process, such as:

* Hope For Orphans—www.hopefororphans.org
* Show Hope—www.showhope.org
* Kingdom Kids Adoption Ministries—www.kingdomkidsadoption.org
* The National Adoption Foundation (NAF)—www.nafadopt.org
* A Child Waits Foundation—www.achildwaits.org

God met our financial needs in ways we never could have imagined. In 2003, we adopted Koyla and reunited him with his best friend.

If you have ever considered adoption and how God might use you and your family as He "places the lonely in families" (Psalm 68:6 NLT), don't let financial fear keep you from being obedient to His call. Some will be called to adopt, and others will be called to support adoption. But the most important things to do are listen to God, follow His lead, and trust His faithfulness.

The financial barriers to adoption can seem overwhelming, but fortunately, we do not have to look at the outward appearance of things; we can look to the One who controls all of the circumstances of our lives.

If a couple feels strongly that God is directing them to adopt and/or to reach out to an orphan, they should begin to save and prepare for the expenses and prayerfully make their needs known to their church, family, and friends. If God truly is leading a couple to adopt, He will be faithful to provide for all of the financial needs.

—Jill Savage

My friends, adoption is redemption. It's costly, exhausting, expensive, and outrageous. Buying back lives costs so much. When God set out to redeem us, it killed Him. And when He redeems us, we can't even really appreciate or comprehend it.

—Derek Loux
Orphan Justice Center and Josiah Fund founder[2]

Prayer Points

Father, adoption can be expensive, but You are Jehovah-Jireh, our Provider. Because we believe You have guided us to adopt, we trust You will provide the means to accomplish Your will. Help us to take good care of the finances You provide. Show us ways to trim current expenses, and guide us to additional funding sources, if necessary. Any sacrifice we make to adopt our child cannot compare to the price You paid to adopt us into Your family. May we keep our eyes on You, trust You, and not waver in our faith.

For a list of additional financing and fund-raising ideas, visit: www.MicheleCScott.com.

Chapter 3

Interceding

July 2005 Orphanage Visit

I could almost hear him calling out to us: "Mommy, Daddy, I love you. I'm here waiting for you. Please come take me home. I need a family. Please."

—Karen Kingsbury[1]

Bathing Your Future Child in Prayer

URING OUR LONG wait for a referral, I decided to pray in detail for our son, like I may have if he were growing in my womb and visible through an ultrasound. Praying this way comforted me amidst the many unknowns, like his name, age, condition, and home-coming date.

> Arise [from your bed], cry out in the night, at the beginning of the watches; pour out your heart like water before the face of the Lord. Lift up your hands toward Him for the lives of your young children.
> —Lamentations 2:19

> A father of the fatherless and a judge and protector of the widows is God in His holy habitation. God places the solitary in families and gives the desolate a home in which to dwell; He leads the prisoners out to prosperity; but the rebellious dwell in a parched land.
> —Psalm 68:5–6

> I will not leave you as orphans [comfortless, desolate, bereaved, forlorn, helpless]; I will come [back] to you.
> —John 14:18

> Although my father and my mother have forsaken me, yet the Lord will take me up [adopt me as His child].
> —Psalm 27:10

> One day children were brought to Jesus in the hope that he would lay hands on them and pray over them. The disciples shooed them off. But Jesus intervened: "Let the children alone, don't prevent them from coming to me. God's kingdom is made up of people like these."
> —Matthew 19:13–15 MSG

> For You did form my inward parts; You did knit me together in my mother's womb. I will confess and praise You for You are fearful and wonderful and for the awful wonder of my birth! Wonderful are Your works, and that my inner self knows right well. My frame was not

hidden from You when I was being formed in secret [and] intricately and curiously wrought [as if embroidered with various colors] in the depths of the earth [a region of darkness and mystery]. Your eyes saw my unformed substance, and in Your book all the days [of my life] were written before ever they took shape, when as yet there was none of them.

—Psalm 139:13–16

One Family's Story: Prayers for Myles and Miles

About two months after beginning our paper pregnancy, my husband, Peter, went to Rwanda for work. He visited the orphanage we would be adopting from. Neither of us had been there during the three years we had lived in Rwanda. I grieved over his descriptions. Knowing that our child and all of the other children were living there without constant attention, touch, and appropriate nourishment, not doted on or celebrated, spun me into two days of near constant grief.

We prayed specifically for Myles to feel touch since he was rarely held or snuggled in a blanket. The fact that he is snugly and affectionate is an answer to our prayers.

—Laurel Greer

"Love From Across the Miles to Myles"
by Bonnie Greer

Little Myles, we think of you
With wonder, trust, and longings too
As first sounds come to infant ears
May they be those that cast out fears.
May others hear your infant cries,
Oh Father, move, that none pass by,
May they wrap you in bunting, tight,
Singing softly, "It's all right."

Do you hear our faith-trust-sigh?
That soon, dear Myles, you'll come nigh?
Little one, what do you see—
Mosquito net or leafy tree?
Oh God of lightness, bring the day,
Keep to him, darkness at bay.
Little one, what do you feel—
The touch of us, for this we kneel?
We pray for those who care for you,
So our embrace won't seem so new.
Little one, our love grows strong,
This lullaby, our hopeful song.
We wait and watch with grateful hearts,
For you, this gift, which God imparts.
Do you hear our faith-trust-sigh
That soon, dear Myles, you'll come nigh?

One Family's Story: What's in a Name

We called our daughter "Chow Chow" (QiaoQiao, her nickname in the orphanage) until she became old enough to prefer Jillian. So when my mom found a baby doll named ChouChou, which we assumed was pronounced the same as our daughter's nickname, Jillian got the doll for Christmas.

Several years and adoptions later, God spoke to my heart about a little girl He had for us. He used many verses, especially "[He] called you out of darkness into His marvelous light" (1 Peter 2:9). I thought that perhaps this child had a special need involving her eyesight.

About that time, an agency posted their new list of adoptable, special needs children from China. This particular agency doubled the children's first names to identify them (LanLan, MeiMei, etc.). To my amusement, I saw a ChouChou posted. She didn't have eyesight problems. She was a heart baby. Because she was darling, I knew she would get a family quickly.

A month or so later, I returned to check the list. I was surprised to see that ChouChou still didn't have a family. I looked at her information again and saw that her heart condition was fairly severe.

For reasons I still do not understand, I called the agency to inquire about her. They told me that a family would be deciding on her over the weekend.

By that time, ChouChou had gripped my heart. I began to pray earnestly for her—and that God would show me if this little girl was our daughter. I sat down at the computer to research her heart condition. As Google brought up the first website, I gasped in utter shock. The slogan on the top of the cardiac site was, "Out of darkness, into light..." I sat rooted to my chair as if a lightning bolt had gone through my body. I thought, *So she is our daughter. But how? We have "too many" kids. There must be another family for her.*

Oddly, my husband, Jeff, who normally needs time to think and pray about another adoption, agreed to ChouChou immediately. I counted the hours until Monday, when I could call the agency.

Monday finally came. So did the news that a different family had stepped forward to adopt little ChouChou. What?! I was crushed. But I didn't insist. She needed surgery and a family who didn't require special permission to adopt beyond the country's family-size limit.

Behind the scenes in China, Love Without Boundaries arranged ChouChou's heart surgery. I kept her picture and surgery date on our fridge as a reminder to pray. A month and a half later, the big day came. I paced and prayed all day. Never had a child so far away touched my heart so deeply.

Later that afternoon, an e-mail appeared with stunning news. Little ChouChou was rejected for surgery and deemed inoperable. Her heart defect was too complicated. They sent her back to the orphanage to be kept comfortable. The family planning to adopt her decided not to continue.

Jeff came home from work to find me crying that ChouChou was going to die. He said calmly, "No she isn't. This only happened so the other family would step out of the way so we can adopt her."

I wasn't connected with Love Without Boundaries then, but I had met the founder, Amy Eldridge, when we both adopted our first children from China. I contacted her to see if ChouChou was indeed unadoptable. I told her we wanted her despite her diagnosis. Amy assured me she would pursue a second opinion and send ChouChou to Hope Healing Home in Beijing to try to improve her health.

To our knowledge, no family had been granted a waiver to the family size rule for about five months. Even so, our agency sent our Letter of Intent to China while we waited at home with baited breath.

Three weeks later, Jeff, along with our son Taylor, headed to Beijing on a missions trip. They planned to visit ChouChou, but since our approval hung in the balance, they tried to stay emotionally distant.

Unbeknownst to anyone but God, I had been begging Him to grant us permission to adopt ChouChou *while* Jeff and Taylor were in China. Meanwhile, in Beijing, the team visited the orphanage. Little ChouChou wanted nothing to do with Jeff or Taylor, strangers with little standing. In two days they would return to the US. I continued to pray fervently.

It was spring break, and I decided to visit my parents, who lived a few hours away. The kids and I were in the van when my cell phone rang.

"Karin? This is the adoption agency."

My heart started to pound. I wanted good news, but what if we had been denied? "Karin, I have your pre-approval!"

I tried not to drive off the road. *"Oh my goodness!!! I can't believe it!! Really?!?!?"*

The minute we got to my parents', I rushed to send an urgent e-mail to the team in China, telling them that Jeff could go back to visit ChouChou, and this time as her daddy.

We found out later that the translator had misspelled her name. It wasn't ChouChou, it was ChaoChao. If it had been spelled correctly, I never would have noticed her on that list. But God knew ChouChou would make a big enough impression to keep me checking on her.

—Karin Prunty

Prayer Points

Lord, we come before You to lift up the needs of our child, whether he/she is developing in his/her birth mother's womb or being cared for in an orphanage or foster family. Hear our prayers for his/her growth, development, and well-being, specifically for his/her:

- *Brain, spinal cord, nerves, and nervous system*
- *Muscles, bones, limbs, and joints*
- *Glands, hormones, and endocrine system*
- *Heart, blood, veins, and cardiovascular system*
- *Immune system and lymphatic system (lymph nodes, spleen)*
- *Nose, throat, lungs, and respiratory system*
- *Mouth, stomach, liver, and digestive system*
- *Kidneys, bladder, and urinary system*
- *Eyes, ears, and skin*
- *Emotional, social, motor, and language development*

If he/she is going to be born soon, we pray for a safe, easy delivery into the world and that he/she will arrive healthy and without any complications. We pray for his/her birth mom—for Your blessing to be upon her for this unselfish gift. Heal her body as well as any grief she may experience as she places her baby for adoption.

If our child is in someone's care at this time, provide him/her with loving and nurturing caregivers. We pray for good nutritional, physical, emotional, and spiritual care. Give him/her opportunities to sleep, play, and exercise. Protect him/her against sickness, injury, and abuse. Heal any hurts or losses he/she may endure. Surround him/her with love, safety, and security now through his/her caregivers and in the future as a member of our family.

Praying for Birth Parents

Let your father and your mother be glad, and let her who bore you rejoice.

—Proverbs 23:25 NKJV

Birth parents deserve our utmost respect. Without their selfless gift of life, there would be no adoption triad to speak of. It's important to pray for our child's first family now and in the years to come.

One Family's Story: The Heart of Adoption

"What are your plans for this baby?" asked the stranger from the travel agency school. "I have a lawyer friend who handles adoptions."

Lisa was a recent high school graduate who was living on her own and who already had chosen life for her baby. The next big decision, who would raise her child, hung in the balance. Lisa herself had grown up without a father. Since she didn't want that for her child, adoption seemed like the best option.

The baby was due on January 12 of the following year, but Lisa's water broke early, on November 28, landing her in the hospital. On the morning of her scheduled discharge, Lisa arose with a stomachache that turned out to be premature labor. Lisa's cries for her mother and her uncle, who would serve as her birth coach, were answered by a nurse's scolding, "Stop crying. You're making things worse."

The nurses in the hall discussed the baby's falling heart rate because of the umbilical cord being wrapped around her neck. Lisa soon underwent an emergency C-section, only to pass out and miss the birth.

Later, Lisa heard reports on her four-pound little girl, who had ten perfect fingers and toes. Confined to her bed for several days, Lisa remained the only one who hadn't seen the baby. She made up for that by returning to the hospital every day to care for the baby girl and check in with Sister Sally, who worked there.

When Lisa arrived at the hospital on December 23, she never anticipated an empty bassinet. Sister Sally explained, "You probably passed her parents in the hall. They came to take her home."

Lisa's heart sank more quickly than a brick in water. She had little choice but to go home empty-handed. She found the strength to get a job and go on with her life, hoping and praying she had made the right decision.

In 2005, nearly twenty years later, Lisa returned from a business trip to a peculiar voicemail. "I believe my niece is your daughter," the woman explained when they spoke by phone. After they confirmed it, the woman continued, "Her mother, Lauren, is here. Would you like to talk to her?"

The two women, connected by their maternal love for the same little girl, expressed their gratitude to each other a dozen times. Toting flowers, Lisa met Lauren the following day. The women enjoyed an instant connection that made words unnecessary.

Lisa glanced down at a picture on the kitchen counter. The girl had long black hair like hers and blue eyes like her birth father. *This must be Allison*, she thought.

Lisa and Lauren spent the next several hours talking and looking through photos. Lisa learned that Allison had lived in the Philadelphia area until moving to North Carolina at age ten. She grew up knowing she was adopted. For her high school senior project, Allison had researched and presented about adoption. She wanted to learn more about her birth mother and hoped to meet her someday. Lauren told Allison about a letter Lisa had written, which they had requested from the lawyer who had facilitated the adoption. The letter brought Allison to tears each time she read it.

Soon Lisa and Allison met by phone, then in person; instantly, they shared a bond. There was a lot of crying and just about every emotion imaginable.

"She was so amazing, so intelligent, and so well-spoken. And she's not even a morning person, just like me. I never thought any of her personality would come from me," Lisa boasted.

After Allison's birth, Lisa experienced health complications and several surgeries. She never was able to have another child. She questioned why God would allow this heartache, but after reuniting with Allison, she knows this was His plan. "It's a miracle. I wasn't prepared for this. It dumbfounded me. We talk at least once a week, and we visit back and forth. We're the best of friends. Every day I thank God. She will always be the biggest accomplishment of my life. I will always be there for her with the biggest open arms. We both know how lucky we are."

—Taken from an interview with birth mother
Lisa Spradling.

Prayer Points

Dear Jesus, I lift up my child's birth family to you. Whether I know them or not, You do. Bless them for their selfless act of love in choosing life for a child they ultimately could not care for. Or, if they lost parental rights, help them overcome the circumstances that led to their family's demise. Guard my and my child's impression of them, helping us to show the utmost respect for their role in our family.

Please give the birth family strength to face life without their child. May they trust You to watch over and care for them. Over the next one, five, ten, twenty, and thirty plus years, free them from any guilt, shame, regret, or condemnation over their decision. Surround them with encouraging people. Comfort them as only You can.

Praying for Others Involved in Adoption

It is better to trust and take refuge in the Lord than to put confidence in man.

—Psalm 118:8

During our lengthy adoption process, I leaned on our agency, social worker, friends, family, and adoptive families online and in our community for encouragement, support, and information. I researched adoption policy news and updates from groups such as the Joint Council on International Children's Services and from trustworthy

Internet sources within Russia. Although the situation and delays were beyond our control, having an understanding of the current events helped me to cope.

Don't hesitate to contact your agency with any concerns you may have. You also can connect with other waiting or adoptive families for support. Visit www.michelecscott.com for a list of resources.

One Counselor's Story: Adoption, a Declaration of Love

Early last fall, the phone rang in a volunteer's home. A client who was expecting had mustered the courage to call our phone line, requesting information on how to plan an adoption. She had called several adoption agencies and was disappointed in what she felt to be a lack of personal caring. She now wanted to plan a private adoption. The client was scheduled to meet with me.

During the months that followed, we developed a very special friendship. First, we explored her options. She had ruled out abortion. Already having had one child, she knew that technically she could parent the baby, yet she was not convinced of that being the best plan.

After weighing resources, relationships, and realities of her current situation, she felt that adoption would benefit all involved. We then explored all of the options within adoption, with her formulating a carefully-laid plan each step of the way. She wanted to provide a stable environment, giving the baby two committed parents. She wanted to select the family and meet them.

Her plans became reality in late fall, when she met face-to-face with the couple she had chosen to raise her baby. Everyone was nervous, each feeling awkward about what to say and what not to say. As often happens, the mutual interests that led her to choose them blossomed into a tender relationship. What began as a brief meeting stretched through the afternoon and into the evening.

The Lord had orchestrated a beautiful plan. I was a spectator, watching it unfold. Besides being coach and cheerleader, my major role was prayer warrior! This client formerly had denied the existence of God, and now she was seeing Him actively involved in what could have been a very negative time of her life.

My work with our client turned toward the technicalities. Desiring a private adoption, she needed to learn how to choose a reputable lawyer and begin that working relationship. We also rolled up our sleeves and began exploring each of her options in planning her upcoming hospital experience. She read designated materials from our library. She wrestled with questions on assigned worksheets. Together we began to explore what she needed to prepare for emotionally. We examined the stages of grieving and how each stage comes into play in an adoption experience. We carefully considered how her family members would be feeling, and even how the parents she had chosen for her child would be feeling. Educational materials were made available to all involved.

All of her hard work was put to the test one Monday in mid-winter. Plans took the back seat, and getting through labor and delivery became the priority. I had the joy of witnessing the miracle of the birth of a precious little boy. Birth grandparents were at the hospital for this big event. At my client's request, the adoptive parents were en route. She invited them into the birthing room as soon as they arrived. Tenderly, she placed the baby in the arms of his adoptive mommy, saying, "Here is your son!" That doubly-loved little boy was snuggled up by members of both his birth family and adoptive family.

At the client's request, provisions were made for the adoptive parents to have primary care of the baby in the hospital. During that time, my client looked at me with awe and said, "I can see God's hand in all of this. I feel so peaceful. This is the way it should be." Later, she repeated that to a close friend, adding, "Working with Patti all this time has really helped. I feel so peaceful."

While in the hospital, we continued to work: exploring options and anticipating the separation when time came to leave the hospital. Tears flowed as signs of healthy emotion, not as indications of regret. Cameras flashed non-stop.

We resumed our appointments at Your Loving Choices in the days and weeks following her delivery. We looked at her goals for rebuilding her life in light of the circumstances that led to her unplanned pregnancy. We examined more closely Whose hand she claimed to have experienced in the hospital.

Planning then turned to focusing on the future court experiences of officially relinquishing her legal rights to parent her son and of willingly transferring those rights to his new parents, whom she herself carefully had chosen. While she and her attorney prepared for the legal process, she and I continued to explore the emotional process and the dynamics of the changing relationships.

Through all of this, one main figure remained peripheral. As the court day approached, I was thrilled to receive a phone call from the baby's absent birth father. He indicated that he personally would like to appear at the courthouse. He had done much heavy thinking, and he now agreed with the birth mother that the adoption plan did provide the most stability for the baby. He wanted to be at court to voice his consent and to prevent the baby from feeling abandoned, as if his birth father did not care.

During a snowy day in late winter, the Lord's loving hand brought together a much-loved little boy, his adoptive mom and dad, his birth mom, and finally, his birth father. Once again, he was snuggled by all who were there. Once again, cameras flashed unceasingly. Once again, I heard my client say, "I feel so peaceful. This is the way it should be."

The heavenly Father is the Author of adoption. His love was evident in every detail through all these months. I spent many hours on my knees, praying through each of those details and for each person involved. I poured out to the Lord my intense emotions as the spectator through all of this. What a privilege! What a joy! Thank You, Lord, for allowing me to work with clients in Your Name!

> —Patti Stoudt on the adoption of Andrew Izzo
> (see Chapter 1)

Prayer Points

Father, we thank you for people working on behalf of orphans and families around the world, including: our agency/attorney; social worker and staff; foreign, domestic, and local government officials, immigration officials, and judges; leaders who influence adoption law and services; orphanage, foster care, and pregnancy center caregivers (both through social services and faith-based programs); churches and ministries; travel agencies, airlines, and hotels assisting adoptive families; adoption watch-dog and children's rights groups; other adoptive families; our family, friends, and support groups who encourage us through the process. We thank you in advance for any doctors, educators (including learning support), and therapists who will work with us on medical, attachment, speech, occupational, physical, and/or emotional needs.

Praying Against Spiritual Warfare

> Prayer is our most formidable weapon, the thing which
> makes all else we do efficient.
>
> —E.M. Bounds[2]

During our adoption process, we ran into several obstacles that tested our faith and challenged our steadfastness. Our agency hinted that we might get a quick referral. No one predicted the months and months of delays caused by adoption policy reviews and changes in Russia. We questioned whether or not a child existed for us.

We filed paperwork in two regions, but we had difficulty receiving updates on our status. What's worse, we were making decisions based on our original time frame. My replacement was hired at the church where I worked, reducing our income. We faced extra paperwork and fees, while our nursery sat empty. What a perfect scenario for the enemy to taunt me with lies. I began thinking that maybe I had misunderstood God's promises and there wouldn't be a baby for us. One day in particular, I cried and threatened to pack up the nursery, asking the Lord why He had saved me just to endure such misery.

Unfortunately, we were tested right up to the day of our son's adoption (after late flights and travel delays jeopardized our court appointment). And then there were the challenges we faced in adjusting to parenthood (see the parenting chapter and the epilogue for details). Through all of this, we learned that prayer provides the armor we need to stand against obstacles before, during, and after the adoption.

> Put on God's whole armor [the armor of a heavy-armed
> soldier which God supplies], that you may be able suc-
> cessfully to stand up against [all] the strategies and the

deceits of the devil. For we are not wrestling with flesh and blood [contending only with physical opponents], but against the despotisms, against the powers, against [the master spirits who are] the world rulers of this present darkness, against the spirit forces of wickedness in the heavenly (supernatural) sphere. Therefore put on God's complete armor, that you may be able to resist and stand your ground on the evil day [of danger], and, having done all [the crisis demands], to stand [firmly in your place].

—Ephesians 6:11–13

I have told you these things, so that in Me you may have [perfect] peace and confidence. In the world you have tribulation and trials and distress and frustration; but be of good cheer [take courage; be confident, certain, undaunted]! For I have overcome the world. [I have deprived it of power to harm you and have conquered it for you.]

—John 16:33

"No weapon formed against you shall prosper, And every tongue which rises against you in judgment You shall condemn. This is the heritage of the servants of the Lord, And their righteousness is from Me," Says the Lord.

—Isaiah 54:17 NKJV

If you make the Lord your refuge, if you make the Most High your shelter, no evil will conquer you; no plague will come near your home.

—Psalm 91:9–10 NLT

Keep a cool head. Stay alert. The Devil is poised to pounce, and would like nothing better than to catch you napping. Keep your guard up. You're not the only ones plunged into these hard times. It's the same with Christians all over the world. So keep a firm grip on the faith. The suffering won't last forever. It won't be long before this generous God who has great plans for us in Christ—eternal and glorious plans they are!—will have you put together and on your feet for good. He gets the last word; yes, he does.

—1 Peter 5:8–11 MSG

The Lord will fight for you, and you shall hold your peace and remain at rest.

—Exodus 14:14

One Family's Story: Perseverance

Even when I walk through the darkest valley, I will not be afraid, for you are close beside me. Your rod and your staff protect and comfort me.

—Psalm 23:4 NLT

The [Russian adoption] process took about two years. During that time, my husband passed away, my nephew passed away, and I broke my leg. I continued with my adoption journey. My son is the best thing that has happened to me, and my husband's family is very much involved. We all love my son.

—Carmela

One Family's Story: A Worthy Cause

My husband and I are foster parents for a Christian adoption agency in Pennsylvania. We adopted our son on December 20, 2004, after fostering him for 1½ years. It was a smooth, easy process, and we were overjoyed!

On April 5, 2005, our agency asked if we would care for an eleven-month-old girl who had suffered severe burns and was being released from the hospital. When we arrived at the burn unit the following day, we knew God had called us to be her forever family. We had cared for many children in foster care in the past, but we had never felt this way about a child, especially since the end goal is normally reunification with the birth family. The hospital staff trained us in wound care and sent us on our way.

Approaching her first birthday, this precious girl weighed only ten pounds and was only twenty-four inches long. Very delayed, she could not hold her head up well, nor could she sit up on her own. But everyone bonded, and she flourished from the love and attention she received. Within two weeks, she could hold her head up, sit up, and pull to a standing position.

Three weeks later, we took her to the local YMCA for a supervised visit with her birth family. Because of her respiratory issues, she couldn't be around anyone who smoked. The birth mom took a smoke break during her one hour visit, and Jayda began to have difficulty breathing. They ended the visit and brought her to us.

We took her to the doctor, where she received breathing treatments and a steroid for home. Later she stayed in pediatric intensive care for twenty days for aspirated pneumonia. She had tubes, wires, and a ventilator attached to her. The doctors warned us that if she lived, she would need a trach before leaving the hospital. But they didn't know our God or how many people were praying.

At that time, "Be still, and know that I am God!" (Psalm 46:10 NKJV) was a special verse to me, and boy did He show us! She survived, didn't require a trach, and began to gain weight—five pounds in one week. Jayda and I had a very special bond after this time in the hospital, which made her two-hour, bi-weekly supervised visits with her birth family difficult for her.

We met her siblings and began to pray about adopting all of the children to keep them together. On September

5th, we learned a great aunt had been approved to raise all three children. Devastated, we continued to pray and trust God to work it out.

A court hearing on October 4th ordered Jayda to move to her aunt's by October 21st. We started dropping her off for three hours twice a week, but the visits were not going well. Her medical needs were not being met, which we reported to the caseworker. Her twin brother and her sister already were there, but due to her medical needs, her move was to be gradual. Her first overnight visit was scheduled for October 14th. I prayed constantly and waited on God to intervene. Our pastor reassured me that we had fulfilled our obligation, caring for her the very best we could, and said that now it was time to let her go.

A friend called me one day with Jeremiah 29:11 (NKJV), "For I know the thoughts that I think toward you, says the LORD, thoughts of peace and not of evil, to give you a future and a hope." Then forty-five minutes before we were supposed to drop Jayda off, the overnight visit was canceled. The other two children were removed from the great aunt's home and returned to their foster home due to safety issues in the great aunt's home.

We continued to pray for God to bring the other children to us, which He did on March 31, 2006. We felt blessed, but it was quite the transition because of emotional issues and developmental delays. The birth parents' rights were terminated on December 18, 2006. However, the birth mom asked that her aunt be considered again as a resource for the children. At the same time, we were sent for a bonding evaluation. The May 2007 report stated the children had no bond with the great aunt and were extremely bonded to us; yet they were required to have weekly supervised visits with the great aunt. They would cry and cling to me, begging me not to make them go.

I thought I could change things on my own by writing to the judge, calling the Department of Public Welfare, and begging the county to reconsider. Nothing worked.

The children began to have nightmares of losing their family. Jayda would pray, "Jesus, please don't take me away from my mommy and daddy." Soon they were sent for overnight visits. How could I explain to two three-year-olds and a five-year-old that they were about to lose the only Mommy, Daddy, and family they had ever known? I finally gave it to God. I pictured laying my three children at His feet and trusting Him to take care of everything. I wondered how I would survive if He decided it was best for my children to move. A calmness came over me, a peace only He could give. I still worried at times, but I knew it was going to be OK.

Through all of this, my husband was a rock. He would reassure me that God had it all under control and that He never would take our babies.

We hired an attorney, and the judge granted us standing, which gave us the right to fight for the children, a first for US foster parents. We went through several court dates over many months while the kids continued their weekly (but not their overnight) visits. All visits stopped on February 1, 2009, because the children were acting out so badly.

Finally, on April 29, 2009, our attorney called to say that we had won the case. Our adoption was finalized on October 28th at 1:45 P.M. at the county courthouse.

We found out that the judge is a born-again Christian and was deeply touched by our case. When we spoke to him at our adoption, he cried and said he knew God wanted these children in our family. He thanked us for fighting and advocating for them. It was the most beautiful adoption!

—Karen Webb

PRAYER POINTS

Lord, the Enemy seeks to discourage us from resting in Your will. We are not surprised by his schemes to prevent this child from becoming a part of our Christian family. He is the father of lies. However, You can expose his lies and confusion, for You are the Light of the world. We look to You for truth, protection, and safety from the Evil One. Dress us for battle, and give us endurance to run the race set before us.

Chapter 4

Waiting

No news yet. Thanks for praying!
>—A handmade button I wore to church one
>Sunday to avoid fielding questions.

ONE THING I can speak about with some authority is waiting. When we submitted our paperwork, we assumed our adoption would be smooth and quick. But the Lord had a different plan in mind which included a child not yet born.

By eighteen months into our adoption journey, I had surpassed my pain and patience thresholds. In a June 2, 2005 e-mail to our agency, I said, "We are frustrated and tired. We have given everything we have, been stretched farther than we ever imagined, and hurt more than anyone will ever know...We've been a 'waiting family' for too long. We're more than ready to board a plane, meet our son, and say 'goodbye' to our *empty* nursery."

"Can You Hear A Mother's Cry?"
A Poem by Michele Cervone Scott

As you look into their faces
Wondering who each one will become
One by one you refer them
To become someone's daughter or son

I wonder
Can you hear a mother's cry
Far across the ocean wide
Until the day she comes to know
When she can bring her dear one home?

You feed, you wipe, you dress them
With tender loving care
Knowing someone, somewhere wants them
And soon they will be there.

I wonder
Can you hear a mother's cry
Far across the ocean wide
Until the day she comes to know
When she can bring her dear one home?

Hearing each case before you
You know there'll be more to come
Children needing families
And parents little ones.

I wonder
Can you hear a mother's cry
Far across the ocean wide
Until the day she comes to know
When she can bring her dear one home?

The wait is long and tiring
But in faith and hope I press on.
Soon our prayers will be answered
And the waiting tears will be gone.

I wonder
Can they hear this mother's cry
Far across the ocean wide
Until the day I come to know
That I can bring my dear one home?

Passing the Time

While the wait was anything but easy, God refined and strengthened us and provided ways to pass the time, including:

- Reading adoption and parenting books
- Seeking and offering encouragement in online forums
- Joining a local adoption support group
- Spending time with friends
- Traveling
- Babysitting
- Completing home projects
- Praying and attending Bible studies
- Starting a lifebook to document our future child's life and adoption

I pray that God, the source of hope, will fill you completely with joy and peace because you trust in him. Then you will overflow with confident hope through the power of the Holy Spirit.

—Romans 15:13 NLT

He grants the desires of those who fear him; he hears their cries for help and rescues them.

—Psalm 145:19 NLT

Weeping may endure for a night, but joy comes in the morning.

—Psalm 30:5b NKJV

[For Abraham, human reason for] hope being gone, hoped in faith that he should become the father of many nations, as he had been promised, So [numberless] shall your descendants be. He did not weaken in faith when he considered the [utter] impotence of his own body, which was as good as dead because he was about a hundred years old, or [when he considered] the barrenness of Sarah's [deadened] womb. No unbelief or distrust made him waver (doubtingly question) concerning the promise of God, but he grew strong and was empowered by faith as he gave praise and glory to God, Fully satisfied and assured that God was able and mighty to keep His word and to do what He had promised. That is why his faith was credited to him as righteousness (right standing with God). But [the words], It was credited to him, were written not for his sake alone, But [they were written] for our sakes too. [Righteousness, standing acceptable to God] will be granted and credited to us also who believe in (trust in, adhere to, and rely on) God, Who raised Jesus our Lord from the dead.

—Romans 4:18–24

So let's not get tired of doing what is good. At just the right time we will reap a harvest of blessing if we don't give up.

—Galatians 6:9 NLT

He has made everything beautiful in its time.

—Ecclesiastes 3:11 NKJV

God's way is perfect. All the LORD's promises prove true. He is a shield for all who look to him for protection.
—2 Samuel 22:31 NLT

If you live in Me [abide vitally united to Me] and My words remain in you and continue to live in your hearts, ask whatever you will, and it shall be done for you.
—John 15:7

But those who wait for the Lord [who expect, look for, and hope in Him] shall change and renew their strength and power; they shall lift their wings and mount up [close to God] as eagles [mount up to the sun]; they shall run and not be weary, they shall walk and not faint or become tired.
—Isaiah 40:31

Wait and hope for and expect the Lord; be brave and of good courage and let your heart be stout and enduring. Yes, wait for and hope for and expect the Lord.
—Psalm 27:14

But if we hope for what we do not see, we eagerly wait for it with perseverance.
—Romans 8:25 NKJV

And therefore the Lord [earnestly] waits [expecting, looking, and longing] to be gracious to you; and therefore He lifts Himself up, that He may have mercy on you and show loving-kindness to you. For the Lord is a God of justice. Blessed (happy, fortunate, to be envied) are all those who [earnestly] wait for Him, who expect and look and long for Him [for His victory, His favor, His love, His peace, His joy, and His matchless, unbroken companionship]!
—Isaiah 30:18

PRAYER POINTS

Father God, waiting for our child may be the hardest stage of this process so far. There are many unknowns, like the timing of the ultimate placement of this child into our family. Help us to find our strength in You when it's difficult to stay strong. Forgive us for doubting or thinking that You don't understand this painful longing. You do understand. You gave us the desire to become parents. And as a parent Yourself, You love each of Your children and long for them to have a relationship with You. May Your promises comfort us and fill us with joy and peace. Take our sadness away, just as You did for Hannah before You blessed her with Samuel. Make us stronger individually and as a couple. Show us how to use this time to prepare our home and our family for this child.

Preparing for the Arrival

Our Nursery – For this child we prayed.

With paperwork, approvals, and financial concerns squared away, it was time to prepare for our baby! I poured over baby item catalogs, websites, *Consumer Reports®*, *Parents®* magazine, and reviews from other families. After years of "expecting," followed by baby shower gifts and hand-me-downs, we actually had accumulated too much baby paraphernalia. Based on our experience, my advice is to only keep the items you need and love, then bless someone else with the rest. Of course, you don't want to forget the following (not all items will apply, especially with older children):

- A first-aid kit, including children's medicines for fever, pain, teething, etc.
- A convenient thermometer (My neighbors recommend the over-the-forehead swipe style that their doctors use.)
- A children's medical reference, such as the book *Take Your Pediatrician With You: Keeping Your Child Healthy at Home and on the Road* by Dr. Christopher S. Ryder, or the KidsDoc Symptom Checker iPhone app from the American Academy of Pediatrics.
- A bath thermometer, towels, washcloths, and no-tears shampoo/body wash
- Toothbrush, toothpaste, comb, brush, and nail clip
- Electric outlet covers and window/cabinet/doorknob locks
- Room and stair gates
- Night light and humidifier
- Smoke alarms
- Batteries in assorted sizes
- Appropriate furniture, bed, and bedding (including a waterproof mattress cover) for the child's room

- Car or booster seat
- High chair and/or booster
- Hamper, hangers, detergent, and fabric softeners
- Infant items (if applicable), such as diapers, diaper cream, changing pad, tub, portable crib, swing, stroller, sling, walker, formula, bottles/sippy cups/straw cups, baby food, dishware, utensils, bibs, etc.

Additional items to pack when traveling are included in the next chapter.

Be sure to check with your insurance company about medical coverage for your soon-to-be child. The insurance company that typically provides resource materials for new parents experiencing pregnancy and birth may offer similar materials for adoptive families. For example, Independence Blue Cross's Healthy Lifestyles initiative includes an Adoption Education Program. I learned about it through a representative at a baby expo when I explained our situation.

> "Don't let this throw you. You trust God, don't you? Trust me. There is plenty of room for you in my Father's home. If that weren't so, would I have told you that I'm on my way to get a room ready for you? And if I'm on my way to get your room ready, I'll come back and get you so you can live where I live. And you already know the road I'm taking."
>
> —John 14:1–4 MSG

> Faith is the confidence that what we hope for will actually happen; it gives us assurance about things we cannot see.
>
> —Hebrews 11:1 NLT

PRAYER POINTS

Gracious Father, You have been faithful to prepare our hearts to receive our adopted child. Now we ask You to prepare our home. Help us to create a safe, loving, and nurturing environment for our child. Lead us to the necessary equipment, furniture, toys, books, and supplies. We thank You for providing the means to care for this child, as well as for our friends' and family's gifts and advice.

Chapter 5

. . . .

Advancing

The Referral

T HE TIMING OF our referral demonstrated how perfect God's timing is! Only, things got worse before they got better.

While we were in the process of waiting for our son, I was unexpectedly relieved from my part-time ministry duties. The same week, my mother was hospitalized and diagnosed with a brain tumor. Devastated, I returned my computer and supplies to the church, feeling prematurely retired. Without the responsibility of children or work, I didn't even stop at the store on my way home from church for fear I'd have nothing to do the following day.

But that very same night—after 1 ½ years in the adoption process—we got the call that would change our lives. We had a son to meet in Russia, good news our family desperately needed! I remember my state of shock and thinking, *We're having a baby! The baby's coming!* and wondering if pregnant women say that when their water breaks.

Information trickled in, such as our son's name, birth date, current and birth measurements, and health status. Without a photo, we consulted over the phone with an international adoption doctor prior to our travel. Meanwhile, we worked frantically to make travel arrangements, finish additional paperwork, and pack. It was a busy and exciting time, with no room to fulfill other obligations. The Lord knew what we needed all along!

> Like cold water to a thirsty soul, so is good news from a far [home] country.
> —Proverbs 25:25

> Don't brag about tomorrow, since you don't know what the day will bring.
> —Proverbs 27:1 NLT

One Family's Story: Fast Track to Family

In March of 2008, my husband, Jon, and I submitted an application to adopt domestically. By the end of June, we had flown through our home study and profile, eager to fulfill our four-year desire for a baby.

The social worker asked one final question before placing us on the waiting list: our race preference. To this point, we had answered "yes" to most of the child criteria questions, with the exception of HIV/AIDS. After praying about the child God had for us, we decided to remain open to any race.

On June 26, 2008, I wrote in my journal, "We are very excited to see what God does and who He brings into our lives. Now it's just the waiting game. My dream is that it will happen fast!!! I'm hoping in less than six months. I am just so very excited to get a baby. Now we just pray and wait."

Exactly one week later, the social worker, Audrey, called me at work. I was working on a patient as a dental hygienist, so I decided to wait until lunch time to return her call, remembering her tip that we would receive many calls before "the call." Perhaps she had a question regarding our upcoming trip to Escanaba on Friday.

"How badly do you want to go to Escanaba?" she asked.

"Not badly. Why? Did someone pick us?"

She said, "Well, actually, there is a beautiful baby girl waiting for you at the hospital!"

I couldn't believe it! I started crying. I went into my office and announced to my coworkers that we'd just had a baby. They were floored and said, "I thought it was a one to two year wait!"

I said, "Me too!" It had been one week!

I told my work I was going to the hospital, and they canceled my afternoon for me. I called Jon and told him we had a baby. He was speechless. He was at a friend's house working on his truck. He rushed home, and we met there.

We went up to the NICU on the 5th floor of the hospital. We showed our I.D.s to the social worker and then washed our hands. Overcome with joy and unbelief, I started bawling. The time finally had come. We turned the corner and walked through another set of doors, went down to the last bassinet on the right hand side, and there was the most beautiful baby girl you ever saw! She was so tiny, weighing in at 6 pounds 5 ounces, and was 19 ¼" long. She was three days old and had thick, black, soft hair, brown eyes, and black skin. She was gorgeous! We named her Ava Mae.

I got to feed her first, and later, Jon fed her. It was then that we realized I had to call my work and tell them I wasn't coming back. My dream of being a stay-at-home mom was becoming a reality. I felt bad about not being able to give them notice; however, there was no way I could work with a little baby needing me at home.

We made a ton of phone calls that day, telling family and friends of our wonderful and extraordinary news. It was hard to leave her at the hospital that night; I did not sleep. The next day we went back up to the hospital, and then later in the day, I went shopping with my mother-in-law and sister-in-law for baby stuff. We spent six hours and over $600 at Babies-R-Us. We needed formula, bottles, a car seat, clothes, a pack-n-play, etc. We didn't even have a room set up for Ava.

We brought Ava home on Thursday at 8:00 P.M., two days after we met her for the first time.

We never met Ava's birth mom, nor did Ava. Her birth mom wanted a traditional adoption initially, so she picked our agency from a list presented to her at the hospital. Audrey went up to meet her. After learning more about the adoption process, Ava's birth mom decided against the traditional way and instead went with a Safe Haven delivery, which meant she wouldn't have to go through all of the court proceedings. The hospital staff gave her another list to choose from for a Safe Haven delivery, and our agency was not on that list. Audrey made a phone call to a judge to add the agency to that list, too. We thank God that Ava's birth mom originally picked our agency and that Audrey was able to get it placed on the Safe Haven delivery list. We could see God working all over this adoption! Ava was officially placed in our home on Friday, May 8, 2009, just two days before Mother's Day.

The greatest challenge we faced through this whole adoption process was fear—fear of someone taking Ava away from us. One thing that helped us with our fear was when Audrey told us, "Regardless of how God brings a child into our lives, He has predetermined the amount of time that child will be in our care." This is true for biological and adopted children. That statement assisted us in recognizing God's role in adoption and helped us to trust Him, regardless of what may come.

—Nanette

One Family's Story: A Perfect Fit

Adoption was always a choice for us. When I was a little girl, I somehow felt the family I was meant to have was going to be built through adoption. I secretly held the desire that my husband and I would adopt, but it seemed to be a lofty goal, especially if we could get pregnant naturally.

After ten years of miscarriages, we decided to seek help. We went to one specialist. It did not seem natural the way he explained it—the mixing of the cells in a petri dish in the back room by the receptionist. To me, that didn't seem like the way that God intended for children to be born. And so we left and never looked back.

After we made the decision to adopt, God was truly in control. We chose an agency that my husband's friends were using for their adoption, but they ended up abandoning the adoption process altogether. It seemed like God had put that desire on their hearts so we could identify the agency.

The next hurdle was the mountain of paperwork and the fluctuating rules Russia had placed on international adoptions. We struggled through it and managed to get our first referral. God had answered our prayers. However, in less than twenty-four hours, the referral fell through. We soon got a second referral, but like the first, it, too, was lost. Then everything stopped. Russia went into restructuring, and the process froze. In my heart I heard the rusty iron curtain fall, and we walled off our hearts. We prayed to God and begged Him to answer why we'd had two beautiful, healthy boys and we'd lost them both. I just kept thinking that if God can move mountains, He can open the Russian wall.

Almost ten months later, Russia opened up, and we received four more referrals, which included a sibling set, a boy and a girl. We considered the siblings, but after our specialist reviewed the video, she had some concerns— concerns we could have dealt with; however, with two children, we needed to be extra careful. The other two were possibilities, but they were outside of the parameters we had given our agency. After much praying and crying, we ultimately turned down all four.

That was a difficult time. Having referrals lost to us was one thing, but to look into the eyes of the children we said no to was something completely different. It broke our hearts, and every day we wondered if we should have said yes. What if God was sending us something beautiful and we had turned it away like it was an old pair of shoes?

Finally, we received our seventh referral, a girl. We were apprehensive and didn't even tell anyone about this referral until we accepted it and had the information reviewed by our medical specialist. Then we slowly told immediate family about the little girl, Alina.

From the moment we accepted her, God validated our choice. Her birth mother's name was my mother's name, Elizabeth. I sat next to a girl at my college graduation— someone whom I never had met—with the name Alina. I stopped by a garage sale, and as I was buying up all of the size 18–24 months girl clothing, I discovered that the garage sale woman's name was Alina! And the list went on.

Two days before we were supposed to come home from our second and final trip to Russia, Alina became sick. She spiked a fever so high she went into seizures: seizures so violent that she shook the bed and woke us up. We were in an apartment, had no contact number for our facilitator, and did not speak a word of Russian. Again, my prayer line went into overdrive. I prayed and prayed so hard for us to find help, for her to be OK, for us to make it through this. We did make it to a crude hospital and were forced to stay overnight. This was probably the first time in my life I lay awake the entire night. I pleaded, begged, and bargained with the Lord to get us through this. He did, and two days later, we were on a direct flight from Moscow to JFK. Again I prayed, one prayer after another, "God…please…no seizures over Greenland…please…no fevers…let us land at JFK…"

I had envisioned a joyous moment when we landed. I was going to take photos of Alina wearing a special outfit and waving a little US flag I had brought. But in reality, when the plane landed, all I did was lie across my daughter's sleeping body and weep. I wept openly and praised God ceaselessly until my husband gently said, "We're home… Oh, and the plane is empty."

God had this adoption in His hands the entire time. We cannot even imagine what would have happened if we had used another agency or accepted one of the other referrals. My husband and I joke that we couldn't have made a more beautiful, funny, smart, kind child than the daughter God Himself created for us.

—Bethany Martin

Prayer Points

Precious Lord, we just received news that we have been matched with a child! Thank You for preserving this life and for giving us this opportunity to become his/ her parents. Guide us in this next phase, when there is much to consider and do! We trust You to handle every detail. Fill us with peace and patience as we wait for the adoption day that will make us a forever family.

Traveling

Eric and Michele Scott in Red Square, Moscow

Once we made our travel arrangements, it became time to pack. I fought the urge to overpack, while making sure we had everything we might need. Here are a few essentials, especially when traveling internationally:

- Mix and match clothing
- An mp3 player with lullabies and speakers
- Plastic storage bags

70

- A few toys
- Snacks
- A list of important addresses and phone numbers related to the adoption and to home
- Adoption and travel documents
- A list of questions to ask caretakers

"Baby Shower Thank You"
by Michele Cervone Scott

We knelt before the Lord one day
To ask Him for a child.
He said that He had heard our prayer
But it might take a while.
And though it's been a journey,
The day has finally come
To travel to a distant land
For the blessing of our son.
So as we celebrate our God,
Who hears and answers prayers
We couldn't forget to thank you, too,
For the ways you've shown you care.
Yes, we've knelt a lot since then
But we haven't knelt alone.
Your faithful prayers have carried us
On our way to bringing him home.

Having traveled to Russia prior to our adoption trips, I was somewhat prepared for the long flight and conditions there. But as the old saying goes, we needed to "expect the unexpected." Sometimes "the unexpected" blessed us, like being able to afford an American hotel because of a discounted adoption rate. I never thought hearing English, eating familiar foods, and enjoying air conditioning would bring tears of gratitude to my eyes. But sometimes "the unexpected" rattled us, like our travel nightmare on our final trip to finalize the adoption and bring our son home.

On that final trip, flight delays from Philadelphia to New York caused us to miss our flight to Moscow. We ran through JFK airport to catch a flight to Paris, France, that would take us to another Moscow flight. Somewhat shaken, we rallied after dinner and the beginning of a movie, until the gentleman behind me had a medical emergency. We landed in Canada, causing a flat tire and a ten plus hour layover for a new tire and crew. We missed that second flight to Moscow, along with our scheduled train to our son's city. At that point, we hoped to make our court appearance.

One day behind schedule, we finally arrived in our son's city a few hours before we had to be in court. We changed into our court attire, got a quick prep for the hearing, and stopped by the orphanage for the required visit with our son before appearing in front of the judge.

The stop to see our son did not go as smoothly as the one when we first met him, but we were too stunned to panic. Once again, we chose to rest in God's plan and His promise to give us a baby.

One Family's Story: Excerpt from a Russian Adoption Journal

February 24: We land in Moscow and are supposed to meet an agency representative. Another couple will be flying in from New York to join us. Alla, our representative, takes us to a car and tells us Vladimir will bring us to the apartment for food, showers, and sleep. We will meet Alla and the other couple at 9:00 P.M. to fly to Rostov on Don. Vladimir takes us to an apartment and introduces us to Zena. She tells us that we are to eat, shower, and then sleep.

At 8:30 P.M., Zena tells us it's time. Vasilli, Zena's husband, is our driver. There are two cars. Ted, Vasilli, and I are in one. The other couple, Alla, and a driver are in the other. We are racing through the Moscow night to catch our plane to Rostov on Don. We meet the other couple, Cindy and Eric from California. Alla tells us we have appointments to see our children tomorrow.

The flight to Rostov on Don is uneventful until we try to land. A snowstorm prevents the pilot from seeing the runway. We are routed to another airport that is 300 miles away. We finally land in the middle of the night. A bus is waiting for us. The buildings look so old that they could have been built before WWI. Alla finds a hotel across the street, but she doesn't know what condition it's in. We walk through the snow to what we hope is a warm, clean bed.

The hotel looks like an old barracks. Our room consists of two cots, a table, a toilet, and a sink. At 5:00 A.M., the hotel floor manager knocks on Cindy and Eric's door and says it's time to go (she says this in Russian, so Cindy and I use our phrase books and hand signals to decipher). We catch the bus and get back on the plane, fingers crossed that this is it. The snow is falling and the plane is being deiced, but we are happy to be on our way again.

February 25: We land in Rostov on Don, gather our luggage, and head to the apartment. We have two drivers and two cars. Sergei is driving Cindy and Eric, and Natasha is driving Ted and me. We are going to stay with a host family in their apartment while we are in Rostov on Don. We have one hour before it's time to meet our children. Ted and I will go with Natasha and Larrissa (our interpreter) to Novocherkassk to see Justin Viktor.

We park in front of a big, gray gate and walk around an old, orange building. We are welcomed by one of the nurses. The director is on her way, and Justin Viktor is sleeping.

The nurse leads us to a sitting area, and then the director/ pediatrician shows up. We go into her office, where I see the couch on which we first saw Justin Viktor sitting in his video. Larrissa and the director copy all of Justin Viktor's documents, and about twenty minutes later, a nurse brings in our son. He has grown a lot since the video. He has a little bit of a cold, but is not at all scared of us.

The representative from the Board of Education has joined us. She will be in court to say we saw Justin Viktor. She asks us if we still want him. Ted and I both say "yes" and "Da." We spend about one hour playing with Justin Viktor and answering and asking questions. We are told that we will receive a schedule of his eating and sleeping habits before we take him home.

Back at the apartment, we finally sleep.

February 26: Today is court day. At 2:30 P.M., Natasha arrives to drive us to the courthouse. In the court room with us are: Larrissa, who acts as our interpreter; the orphanage director, who will represent Justin Viktor; the Board of Education representative (a social worker), who will represent Justin Viktor; the region prosecutor, who ensures all paperwork and procedures were completed as required; a court stenographer; and the judge.

The judge is a woman in her forties or fifties, in a black robe, and very serious. She announces that we are all here to discuss the petition of Charles and Jennifer Greenman to adopt Viktor Chaikin. She asks us to give our names, birth dates, and address. She asks Ted about fifteen to twenty questions while she reviews our documents. The Board of Education representative is asked to speak. She states that no Russian couples are waiting to adopt a child of this age. She mentions that she was present during our visit with Justin Viktor and that he did not cry in our presence.

Now the orphanage director stands up and discusses Justin Viktor's health, that he is a calm baby, and that he is eligible for us to adopt. The prosecutor confirms all paperwork has been completed appropriately and in the correct timeframes. The judge then goes through our dossier and announces the content page by page.

The judge asks if we have any other petitions before the court? Ted says we would like to waive the ten-day waiting period so that our doctor can see Justin Viktor as quickly as possible and so that Justin Viktor can celebrate his first birthday with his family in America. The Board of Education representative states she has no issues with waiving the waiting period. The orphanage director states she supports waiving the waiting period because having us visit every day for the next ten days would be disruptive to her orphanage. The judge states she will take some time to review the case and then will return with the court's decision on both petitions.

Within about ten minutes (but it seemed a lot longer), the judge returns with her decision. The court has granted our petition for adoption and our petition to waive the ten-day waiting period. She congratulates us and then leaves the room. Ted and I hug each other, Larrissa, the orphanage director, and Alla, when she joins us.

On the way back to the apartment, Larrissa explains that we will not have Justin in our custody until we can hand the orphanage director all of the finalized documents. She expects this to be late Wednesday or early Thursday. Then we will fly to Moscow for the US Embassy approval. Ted and I are relieved that the court decision is made.

February 28: At 9:30 A.M., Natasha takes us to pick up Justin. When we get to the orphanage, the director gives us one of Justin's shirts, a box of cereal, and his schedule. Justin smiles when he sees us. As we walk out of the orphanage, all of Justin's caregivers come to say good-bye to him.

Justin has been very alert since we picked him up. He hasn't cried or whimpered. He sucks his thumb and holds his hands together when he feels nervous or scared. We are flying back to Moscow tonight, at 6:40 P.M.

March 3: We leave Moscow at 4:00 A.M. It's still dark out, and there is very little traffic. Snow is falling. Vladimir helps us get through the security check and with our declaration forms. Once we take off, the flight is uneventful.

We arrive in Paris fifteen minutes before our connecting flight is supposed to leave. We rush to our gate but are too late. Ted arranges for us to catch a flight to Newark, NJ, the closest destination that Ted can get to Philadelphia. We cannot stay overnight in Paris because Justin's visa only allows him to enter the US—not any other countries. I call my parents with the change in plans.

When we land in Newark, we go straight to immigration and beat the crowd. It takes about ten minutes for Justin to gain access to the United States. Immigration keeps everything in the packet—we never get to see what is in it.

When we see Wyatt, he yells, "My brother has blond hair!" I put Justin in the car seat next to Wyatt, and they hold hands until Justin falls asleep. I am so happy.

—Jennifer Greenman

Lean on, trust in, and be confident in the Lord with all your heart and mind and do not rely on your own insight or understanding. In all your ways know, recognize, and acknowledge Him, and He will direct and make straight and plain your paths.

—Proverbs 3:5–6

"Instantly"
A Poem by Michele Cervone Scott

How can I comprehend what I am about to see?
The years of waiting now becoming a memory.
Your eyes, your skin, your hair. Oh, the wonder of your face!
I can't believe this day we have finally embraced!

Instantly, the pain I felt so deeply has now gone.
Instantly, I have a child to call my very own.
Instantly and suddenly, you are my dream come true.
Instantly, so instantly, I have been blessed with you.

I hardly can believe it, how beautiful you are!
Practically perfection, the most precious one by far.
A gift that was tucked away until this very day
That we could meet; I feel complete knowing you're OK.

Instantly, the pain I felt so deeply is now joy.
Instantly, I now have met my handsome little boy.
Instantly and suddenly, you are my dream come true.
Instantly, so instantly, I have been blessed with you.

How can I begin to thank my Father up above
For allowing me to know the depth of mothers' love?
Tears I've cried before this day don't matter anymore.
There's joy in my heart from the start that was not there
      before.

Instantly, a good, perfect gift was bestowed on me.
Instantly, we get to share now 'til eternity.
Instantly and suddenly, you are my dream come true.
Instantly, so instantly, I have been blessed with you.

I will try my very best to love and care for you.
That's what your other mom would have wanted me to do.
A responsibility and honor to enjoy,
Molding you into a man from just a little boy.

PRAYER POINTS

Domestic travel to receive your child:

Lord, we are about to travel to complete our domestic adoption. We are grateful for this opportunity and ask You to guide each step. Give us peace to handle details in the midst of excitement and anxiousness. Help us to pack the right items for ourselves and our child and to remember necessary items like currency, paperwork, and contact numbers. Please keep us safe as we travel. Provide opportunities to show Your love to the people we meet. Help us to be sensitive and respectful. We look to You for wisdom and clarity during this important trip for our family.

International travel to receive your child:

Lord, we are about to travel to another country to complete our international adoption. We are grateful for this opportunity and ask You to guide each step. Give

Noah and Daddy in our Moscow hotel lobby.

us peace to handle details in the midst of excitement and anxiousness. Help us to pack the right items for ourselves and our child, without forgetting necessary items like passports, visas, currency, paperwork, and contact numbers. Show us which over-the-counter medicines and convenience items are not readily available outside of this country. Prevent us from weighing ourselves down with unnecessary items and luggage. Keep us safe as we travel by plane and any other means here and abroad. Provide opportunities to show Your love to the people we meet, regardless of language barriers. Help us to show respect and flexibility as visitors to this country, especially if problems occur. We look to You for wisdom and clarity during this important trip for our family.

Your child's travel to you:

Lord, our child is about to travel to join our family. We are grateful for this opportunity. Help ease our child's fears as he/she leaves familiar surroundings and travels here. Keep our child and his/her escort safe as they travel. We pray for complete peace as we await our child's arrival to our family.

Chapter 6

Parenting

Behold, I tell you a mystery: We shall not all sleep, but we shall all be changed.

—1 Corinthians 15:51 NKJV,
taken out of context for humor

Bonding time between Noah and Daddy

Adjustment

> Relax my dear, your little elf
> Is just an amateur herself.
> So if your hands so newly filled
> With tasks seem somewhat less than skilled
> Relax, I say, this little pinkling
> Doesn't have the slightest inkling
> That you are new to baby lore…
> She never had a mom before.
> —Title and Author Unknown[1]

THE LONG-AWAITED MOMENT, welcoming our son home, finally arrived. We packed the diaper bag with the cutest outfit and a wide-range of essentials before heading off to the orphanage.

With sunshine, blue skies, and cottony clouds overhead, we entered the orphanage with complete confidence in our parenting abilities. We opened our arms. Noah opened his. He cried, "Mommy!" I replied, "Son!" as heart-warming music played in the background. I couldn't have asked for a more picture-perfect moment to include in Noah's lifebook…

And now for the real story. We probably bit our nails all the way to the orphanage. Our diaper bag, which rivaled a climber's pack for Mt. Everest, housed every infant remedy and necessity known to man, except the picture-perfect welcome home outfit that I forgot to pack. With little choice, I handed the orphanage worker an ordinary change of clothes that will someday grace his lifebook.

We looked at Noah with a mixture of joy and trepidation that matched his deer-in-headlights expression. We gave the caregivers gifts. They presented a pink phone (yes, I said pink) to Noah to remember the orphanage by, and we headed back to the hotel, breaking our first rule in parenting—no car seats are required in Russia.

We hardly got settled at the hotel before our translator sprang Noah's daily schedule and typical menu on us, like the eggs he'll never eat for me. We played, read books, and crawled around the non-baby-proofed hotel room while Eric and our translator went to complete paperwork. Oh, yeah, and we pushed buttons on the pink phone.

Fast forward several days of diapers, formula, and sleepless nights. We traveled by overnight train to Moscow and spent several days cooped up in an American hotel, away from the disapproving eyes of some Russians watching shell-shocked couples caring for their newly-adopted, soon-to-be-leaving Russian children.

To our surprise, we flew home to Pennsylvania without incident. After our long day of traveling, we requested no fanfare or crowds with signs like the ones seen on *An Adoption Story*. Instead, my parents and our good friend Amy greeted us with hugs and smiles.

Already guarding the nest, we sent everyone home so the three of us could settle in as a family. But jet lag and new-parent-induced tension mounted from about the time we walked through the door. We pondered whether or not Noah should sleep in his crib or in our room in the pack and play? I decided on the pack and play, which was set up downstairs. Not knowing how to collapse it, Eric dragged it up the steps, banging it into the walls and railing. I got upset. I think Noah was upset, too, and thus started our first night of happy transition to home.

Over the next few days, we took Noah to see the pediatrician and for blood work (without any shoes, by the way) and to meet Amy's kids (the few "cousins" he'll ever know.) We also welcomed both sets of grandparents for visits while fighting to overcome jet lag.

Within a week, Eric returned to work, leaving me in tears as I tried to figure out this stay-at-home mother thing. I remember my first errands alone with Noah. At that time, our bank and post office were just a few parking lots away from each other. We pulled up to the bank, got out, went through the line, and went back to the car. We arrived at the post office, got out, went through the line, and returned to the car. In and out of the car seat three times was enough for me to call it a day.

On another outing, this time to the grocery store, I couldn't lift Noah out of the shopping cart. When an older woman came over to help me, I explained that I was a new adoptive mom, for fear of looking like a complete idiot.

A month or two later, I brought Noah with me to my doctor's appointment. The nurse kept asking him, "Where did you get that blond hair?"

When she wouldn't stop (he hadn't learned to talk yet), I answered, "His father had blond hair like that when he was little." It was the truth. I just didn't mention which father or feel obligated to comment on our adoption. I actually was tempted to say I didn't know who his father was, just to be funny (and also true—the birth father), but I figured it was better to avoid any appearance of promiscuity on this particular occasion.

Ah, the things they neglected to teach us in our pre-adoptive parenting classes…

One Family's Story: Mother-to-Mother Wisdom

Dear Michele,

You have been blessed with a wonderful baby, Noah.

Babies don't come with instructions—it's all trial and error. He will be happy, bouncy, joyful,

and also crabby, cranky, and irritable—just like all
people. His problem is he can't talk and tell you his
problem—diaper, nap time, or hunger.

Dad and I are available 24/7 for help, for advice
(wanted or unwanted), and to comfort when tears
are the only release. Michele, I have always told you
to cry when you feel the need. It releases tension.
We all need to release tension.

I would feel needed and appreciated to clean,
vacuum, do floors, change beds, go to the laundro-
mat, whatever! Dad can help also. Don't feel like you
and Eric must do it all. All new parents need help.
The smart ones aren't afraid to ask.

Love,
Mom
(Betty Ann Cervone)

I wish I had taken Mom's advice sooner. They were a big
help, but I was too overwhelmed to realize I needed more.
We also received help with meals and cleaning. Still, I stared
at laundry piles, dirty dishes, and a screaming child and felt
defeated. Was this really the life I signed up for?

"Before I Was A Mom"[2]
Author Unknown

Before I was a Mom,
I made and ate hot meals.
I had unstained clothing.
I had quiet conversations on the phone.
Before I was a Mom,
I slept as late as I wanted
And never worried about how late I got into bed.
I brushed my hair and my teeth everyday.

Before I was a Mom,
I cleaned my house each day.
I never tripped over toys or forgot words of lullabies.
Before I was a Mom,
I didn't worry whether or not my plants were poisonous.
I never thought about immunizations.
Before I was a Mom,
I had never been puked on
Pooped on
Spit on
Chewed on
Peed on
Or pinched by tiny fingers.
Before I was a Mom,
I had complete control of:
My thoughts
My body
And my mind.
I slept all night.
Before I was a Mom,
I never held down a screaming child
So that doctors could do tests
Or give shots.
I never looked into teary eyes and cried.
I never got gloriously happy over a simple grin.
I never sat up late hours at night watching a baby sleep.
Before I was a Mom,
I never held a sleeping baby just because I didn't want to
    put it down.
I never felt my heart break into a million pieces
When I couldn't stop the hurt.
I never knew that something so small
Could affect my life so much.
I never knew that I could love someone so much.
I never knew I would love being a Mom.
Before I was a Mom,
I didn't know the feeling of having my heart outside my body.

I didn't know how special it could feel to feed a hungry baby.
I didn't know that bond between a Mother and her child.
I didn't know that something so small
Could make me feel so important.
Before I was a Mom,
I had never gotten up in the middle of the night every ten
    minutes to make sure all was OK.
I had never known the warmth
The joy
The love
The heartache
The wonder
Or the satisfaction of being a Mom.
I didn't know I was capable of feeling so much
before I was a Mom.

I didn't know much about being a mom, but I knew about becoming one. So when it came time for our "happily ever after," that's what I expected. Instead of enjoying every diaper change (if that's possible), feeding, or toy, I felt compelled to be the perfect mom our home study promised.

A million thoughts and fears overwhelmed me. *Am I doing this right? Will Noah learn to trust us? Can I make up for the year Noah went without a mom?* I was scared to voice the thoughts, for fear I'd seem ungrateful or be reminded of how long I'd prayed for him. Even worse, I worried that I would make a mistake and the agency would take him back.

At the same time, I felt lonely and tired. For the first three months, I built an imaginary moat around our family to promote healthy attachment. Then we added another month while Noah recovered from his circumcision surgery.

I missed my old life, especially sleeping and showering regularly, which also made me jealous of Eric. I wanted to work, run errands, and feel accomplished, not sit isolated at home on a baby's two-nap schedule. Where were the friends, park dates, and playgroups I had fantasized about? And why did I throw our paperwork and photos in a box instead of scrapbooking each memory?

I loved our little boy, but motherhood was harder than I had anticipated. I found myself telling people, "Noah's doing great, but I'm still adjusting." He seemed active and happy—a stark contrast to my mood swings, crying, and irritability. But he also got a stressed look on his face at times as if the energy inside of him was about to explode. He would jump on us and on the furniture. Some people dismissed my concerns about this, stating that he was just being a boy, but my gut instincts disagreed. Later, we discovered his undiagnosed food sensitivities and sensory issues. These challenges were in addition to the speech and developmental delays that already had been detected.

Ten months after Noah's homecoming, I told my OB-GYN how emotionally drained and weepy I had been. She prescribed Zoloft for anxiety and post-adoption depression. I also sought help from an attachment specialist, who evaluated us and talked through the rough patches with me. With a clearer head and my emotions in check, I felt better able to handle my stay-at-home-mom responsibilities.

After speaking with our social worker and other adoptive families, I've learned how difficult post-adoption adjustment can be for families. That's why I developed the PULSE system to provide simple strategies for post-adoption success:

P = *Am I letting go of Perfection?*

- Problem: We have unrealistic expectations.
- Solution: Catch and correct faulty thinking. Give yourself permission to learn.

U = *How can I gain better Understanding?*

- Problem: Parenting is a tough job with various responsibilities and challenges.
- Solution: Gather info from books, professionals, other parents, and prayer to help you parent your child. Then trust your instincts, especially when it comes to well-meaning friends and family members who don't understand the unique aspects of adoption.

L = *Am I taking time to Love?*

- Problem: We can get caught up in the job and not the joy of parenting.
- Solution: Take time to enjoy your child. Play, cuddle, or take a walk. In other words, fake it until you feel it.

S = *Where can I turn for Support?*

- Problem: We don't always know what we need.
- Solution: Solicit help ahead of time (meals, laundry, housework, playtime while you take a nap), have help standing by, and utilize local resources (nursery schools, grocery store or fitness center babysitting, etc.) And don't feel guilty...breaks make better moms!

E = *Where can I find Encouragement?*

- Problem: We don't pat ourselves on the back enough or believe the compliments we receive.
- Solution: Take credit for good parenting choices. Keep a special verse nearby to brighten your mood. Acknowledge that you are your child's patient, loving advocate.

We didn't know about all of the blessings and challenges God had planned for our family, but we wouldn't trade one of them. I pray the same is true for you as you continue on your journey and welcome your children home.

> I will never forget this awful time, as I grieve over my loss. Yet I still dare to hope when I remember this: The faithful love of the Lord never ends! His mercies never cease. Great is his faithfulness; his mercies begin afresh each morning. I say to myself, "The Lord is my inheritance; therefore, I will hope in him!" The Lord is good to those who depend on him, to those who search for him.
>
> —Lamentations 3:20–25 NLT

> The LORD opens the eyes of the blind. The LORD lifts up those who are weighed down. The LORD loves the godly. The LORD protects the foreigners among us. He cares for the orphans and widows, but he frustrates the plans of the wicked.
>
> —Psalm 146:8–9 NLT

> I know the one in whom I trust, and I am sure that he is able to guard what I have entrusted to him.
>
> —2 Timothy 1:12b NLT

> Therefore humble yourselves [demote, lower yourselves in your own estimation] under the mighty hand of God, that in due time He may exalt you, Casting the whole of your care [all your anxieties, all your worries, all your concerns, once and for all] on Him, for He cares for you affectionately and cares about you watchfully.
>
> —1 Peter 5:6–7

> The Lord God is my Strength, my personal bravery, and my invincible army; He makes my feet like hinds' feet and will make me to walk [not to stand still in terror,

but to walk] and make [spiritual] progress upon my high
places [of trouble, suffering, or responsibility]!
—Habakkuk 3:19

One Family's Story: When Everything Changes

We have two birth children, Evan (twelve years old)
and Lila (nine years old), and one adopted child, Jeremy
(eight years old.) Jeremy was adopted from an Asian country
because my mother-in-law is Asian. My husband was born
in the US and always has lived here, but we felt the ethnic
connection would be important. Once our paperwork
reached the country, it "sailed through," perhaps because
of my husband's ethnicity.

Jeremy was eighteen months old at the time and in a
Christian orphanage with lots of love. The orphanage got
Jeremy right out of the hospital and kept very good records.
We have pictures of him from birth until we picked him
up. We also have pictures of his birth mother, his half
sister, and those who cared for him at the orphanage.
The social worker there even had his birth mother write
a letter to him.

Jeremy was perfectly happy at the orphanage. We met
him on a Monday and took him on a Tuesday. This dramatic
separation, along with the initial separation from his birth
mother, most likely has caused him to have high anxiety.

We took Jeremy home. It was a very difficult adjustment
for everyone. Jeremy has an intense personality, and he
screamed for the first three years he was home with us.
Our other two children were excited at first, but then they
found him very difficult to be around and that he was taking
almost all of my (Mom's) attention.

Six months after arriving in the US, we moved to the
Midwest to be near my family. These were a lot of transitions

for Jeremy (as well as for the entire family), and we struggled for a few years.

My husband and I began to realize that Jeremy's domination of the household was more than just adjustment and his intense personality. So we brought him to be evaluated for emotional issues, and the response was that he is just devious. We adjusted his diet a few times. (We already have a very healthy diet, eating mostly organic food and very little artificial colors and preservatives, etc.)

Throughout all of this, our marriage suffered, and our other two children suffered as well. I worked hard to shield them from Jeremy's difficult behaviors. But the addition of Jeremy to our home had changed Evan and Lila. I could see this happening but was so overwhelmed myself that I couldn't find a way to make it any easier for them.

My husband became more and more frustrated and angry at Jeremy's domination of our family. My husband had been diagnosed with depression previously in his life but was able to function well without medication. However, he is now on anti-depressants to ease the difficulties of parenting Jeremy.

We continued to seek professional help. For over a year now, Jeremy has been in play therapy with a wonderful Christian therapist who has helped us greatly in our parenting of him. After a few initial meetings, she said that there is hope, but healing will take a *long* time. Also, Jeremy went through more psychological testing and has been diagnosed with high anxiety and ADHD. After many tears and much trying of different medications, he is now on Prozac and another drug for ADHD. These have helped a lot, but they are not magic bullets.

My advice to potentially adoptive parents is the following:

1. Both parents need to be equally supportive and desiring of the adoption. If things become difficult, one may blame the other.
2. Be financially prepared to pay for therapy or doctors out-of-pocket. We are paying about $300 a month for Jeremy's therapy. This will continue for a long time.
3. Do not take things personally as your adoptive child begins to learn about his/her unique journey. My son tells me often that I don't love him and that he's stupid. Emotionally, he is about eighteen months behind those his age, so statements he says in public or private can be hurtful if I let them.

Despite all of this, we do love our son. He is incredibly smart and creative and can be lots of fun. We have been challenged like we never thought possible. The Lord has been shining a light on the dark places of our hearts we didn't know existed. Both my husband and I didn't realize how much anger was in both of us. The passage from James 1:19–20 (NKJV) has convicted us greatly: "So then, my beloved brethren, let every man be swift to hear, slow to speak, slow to wrath; for the wrath of man does not produce the righteousness of God."

At our church, we have a small support group of families with special-needs children, and the children are all adopted. It's important for people to realize that adopted children have special needs. One book that has been of great help through the struggles is *Twenty Things Adopted Children Wish Their Adoptive Parents Knew* by Sherrie Eldridge. I would highly recommend this book to anyone who is thinking about adoption or has already adopted.

We don't know what the future holds. Our son is the type to try things (alcohol, drugs, etc.) just because they are there. However, we know we cannot control events, so our trust is in the Creator of the universe. We are learning to a greater extent to take life one day at a time.

—Anonymous

PRAYER POINTS

Heavenly Father, as the proud parents of our adopted child, we can't thank You enough for this awesome gift. What a privilege it is to call this child our own. Thank You for guiding us through the adoption process and for making us a family. We look to You for the wisdom and strength needed in parenting. It is a great responsibility that we do not take lightly. Help us to be sensitive to our child's background, and give us wisdom as we seek to meet his/her physical and emotional needs. Show us how to love our child. Help us to form an intimate bond. Please remove any obstacles to attachment, and do not allow the enemy to hinder us in any way. We have many opportunities to gain insights from books, family members, and friends. Yet we ask for Your direction as we train, discipline, and nurture the child You have given us.

Beyond Adjustment

Some are kissing mothers and some are scolding mothers, but it is love just the same, and most mothers kiss and scold together.

—Pearl S. Buck[3]

Being a parent is such an awesome responsibility. There is much to do, much to learn, much adjusting, and even mistakes to be made. I have learned that it's essential to go with the flow, trust your instincts, and claim God as your covering. Thankfully, children are very forgiving!

At some point, whether it is one month, one year, or more, you will sigh with relief that your family has adjusted to your new addition. And the parenting journey continues.

People tend to make the act of adopting a child idealistic and like it's going to be this forever ever after, warm walk in the sunshine, and you know what? Raising children today, whether or not you're raising adopted children or biological ones, it's a challenge. It is an absolute challenge.

—Dennis Rainey[4]

For our earthly fathers disciplined us for a few years, doing the best they knew how. But God's discipline is always good for us, so that we might share in his holiness. No discipline is enjoyable while it is happening—it's painful! But afterward there will be a peaceful harvest of right living for those who are trained in this way.

—Hebrews 12:10–11 NLT

Fathers, do not irritate and provoke your children to anger [do not exasperate them to resentment], but rear them [tenderly] in the training and discipline and the counsel and admonition of the Lord.

—Ephesians 6:4

It is not that we think we are qualified to do anything on our own. Our qualification comes from God.

—2 Corinthians 3:5 NLT

Give yourselves to disciplined instruction; open your ears to tested knowledge.

—Proverbs 23:12 MSG

Do not withhold correction from a child.

—Proverbs 23:13 NKJV

And all your [spiritual] children shall be disciples [taught by the Lord and obedient to His will], and great shall be the peace and undisturbed composure of your children.

—Isaiah 54:13

If you don't know what you're doing, pray to the Father. He loves to help. You'll get his help, and won't be condescended to when you ask for it.

—James 1:5 MSG

Finally, brethren, whatever things are true, whatever things are noble, whatever things are just, whatever things are pure, whatever things are lovely, whatever things are of good report, if there is any virtue and if there is anything praiseworthy—meditate on these things. The things which you learned and received and heard and saw in me, these do, and the God of peace will be with you.

—Philippians 4:8–9 NKJV

And you must love the LORD your God with all your heart, all your soul, and all your strength. And you must commit yourselves wholeheartedly to these commands that I am giving you today. Repeat them again and again to your children. Talk about them when you are at home and when you are on the road, when you are going to bed and when you are getting up.

—Deuteronomy 6:5–7 NLT

And He said to them, "Come aside by yourselves to a deserted place and rest a while." For there were many coming and going, and they did not even have time to eat.

—Mark 6:31 NKJV

And I will give them one heart and one way, that they may [reverently] fear Me forever for the good of themselves and of their children after them.

—Jeremiah 32:39

My child, listen when your father corrects you. Don't neglect your mother's instruction. What you learn from them will crown you with grace and be a chain of honor around your neck.

—Proverbs 1:8–9 NLT

Dear child, if you become wise, I'll be one happy parent. My heart will dance and sing to the tuneful truth you'll speak.

—Proverbs 23:15–16 MSG

PRAYER POINTS

Abba Father, parenting is a multi-faceted job, and You know the joy and the pain it brings. You declared Your pleasure over Your Son, Jesus, from the heavens, and You watched Him suffer on the cross so we might be saved.

Give us a constant supply of wisdom and strength as we face the challenges of raising a child. We thank You for our forever family, which we entrust to Your care.

Chapter 7

Supporting

I had this mistaken notion that when we adopted our daughter that I would be able to influence her and guide her and direct her, and we have, to a degree, but I did not understand, and I underestimated that adopted children and babies and little ones when they're adopted are not blank slates.

—Barbara Rainey[1]

Unique Needs

Each child comes into a family with a unique set of needs, and I think because of being adopted, I think an adopted child has a unique set of needs as well.

—Michael Easley[2]

PARENTING BRINGS ITS share of challenges to all moms and dads, no matter who their children are. But add rough starts, developmental delays, broken homes, and even abuse, and it can become a long, seemingly-endless road to "happily ever after."

The idea of support for an adoptive family is two-fold: supporting the child through the difficulties of life and supporting the parents who are supporting the child. My husband and I never hesitated to get Noah any and every help he needed. We scheduled Noah's evaluation with our county's Early Intervention program as well as a physical exam with a pediatrician before we even left for Russia.

Someone told me that "special kids get special moms." I never felt that special, nor did I believe God thought so either. But dealing with a special needs child meant we were parents with special needs. Fortunately, none of our friends and their children were dealing with atypical issues at that time. The therapists and professionals working with Noah provided tips and resources, but we sought additional support from social workers, counselors, websites, online forums, and other adoptive parents for the encouragement that we weren't alone.

To this day, Noah receives learning support, speech therapy, occupational therapy, and extended school year services. From time to time, we've concentrated on specific areas, like social skills and feeding preferences. My mother-in-law boasts that if there's a therapy or program to address an issue Noah has, I will find it. And I'm proud to wear that badge of honor. Although it did take several years and therapies (for both of us) before I was able to embrace Noah's quirks and delays.

One example of my growth in this area comes from when Noah's three-year-old preschool class did a performance. On parent days, I would get extra sensitive because Noah did not sing or participate like the majority of his classmates. This time, however, I made a conscious decision to smile the biggest smile regardless, as if Noah were singing the loudest.

Another example happened in line at a fast-food restaurant, well after we'd started occupational therapies and a dye-free diet. Noah was especially hyper that day, which seemed to annoy the child-free, working couple in front of us. I ignored their whispers and stares, unapologetic for Noah or his needs. After all, I didn't owe them an explanation, but I did owe Noah the mom he waited for and who waited for him.

Yes, we're dealing with needs that require special techniques. We put off potty training until right before Noah turned four. I avoid vacuum cleaning when he's home because of the noise. And we've got more meetings, evaluations, reports, and therapists than I'd care to admit.

Truth be told, being a strong, effective parent, caregiver, and advocate is an ongoing challenge. I never know how a public event, new school year, IEP (Individualized Education Program) meeting, or parent-teacher conference will affect me. But my goal is always the same—to use prayer and action to promote my child's successful development.

In an earlier chapter, I quoted the poem "Before I Was a Mom." Here is my addendum in regards to dealing with special needs:

> Before I was a mom,
> I didn't know a speech delay could be frustrating.
> I didn't know kids with sensory issues could be extra
>   sensitive to light and sounds or require deep pressure,
>   occupational therapy, and a special diet.
> I didn't know food additives could make a child hyper and
>   a mommy yell.
> But before I was a mom,
> I didn't know the joy of looking at the world through
>   different eyes.
> I didn't know the "special" of a special needs mom.
> Life seemed easier because no one depended on me for his
>   every need.
> Now that I'm a mom,

My hands might be full,
But you should see my heart.

Anyone who meets a testing challenge head-on and
manages to stick it out is mighty fortunate. For such
persons loyally in love with God, the reward is life and
more life.

—James 1:12 MSG

And God *is* able to make all grace abound toward you,
that you, always having all sufficiency in all things, may
have an abundance for every good work.

—2 Corinthians 9:8 NKJV

And this same God who takes care of me will supply all
your needs from his glorious riches, which have been
given to us in Christ Jesus.

—Philippians 4:19 NLT

You will keep him in perfect peace, Whose mind is stayed
on You, Because he trusts in You.

—Isaiah 26:3 NKJV

The LORD is good, a strong refuge when trouble comes.
He is close to those who trust in him.

—Nahum 1:7 NLT

One Family's Story: There's No Place Like Home

We adopted our daughter from Vietnam when she was
four months old. We bonded with her immediately and felt
lucky to have such a cute, healthy, and smart baby with
such a spunky personality! I often wondered if I loved her
so much because she was so special or just because she was
my daughter.

As she grew older, I never tired of looking at her beautiful face. Strangers even turned heads as they passed her.

Then, at the age of five, when she lost her hair and was deathly pale from chemotherapy, I knew I loved her simply because she is my daughter. When she was first diagnosed with cancer, I thought, *This cross is too heavy for me to carry!* But God felt close the entire time. He understood our suffering completely.

God wanted us to be her parents. We live only twenty minutes from the best children's hospital in the country, if not in the world, and I work there. What kind of medical care might our daughter have received had she stayed in Vietnam? My husband is also a medical professional, so he was able to give her injections at home. Because of good medical care, she is now in remission and has minimal side effects from her surgery and chemotherapy.

—Anonymous

One Family's Story: A Lesson in Faith

I'll never forget the coos and cries from down the hall as we and the other families waited to meet our Chinese daughters. One by one, they announced our babies' names. Then I heard, "Ling Guang Yi." I almost grabbed my new daughter out of the director's arms.

Tiny and fragile, Laura didn't cry. But she bounced up and down on my lap, appearing to balance herself on her legs. "Oh, my, she's going to keep us moving," I giggled. Some parents watched our quiet Laura, seeming to wish their daughters would stop crying.

We and the other families returned to the hotel to feed, bathe, and dress our new additions. Laura took her bottle well and whined during her bath. After we dressed and held her, she seemed content. But then the honeymoon ended.

Laura never made another sound, except for a repetitive whining at night or one fierce cry before vomiting her new formula. And she didn't move or attempt to interact with anyone or anything.

My husband, Jamie, suspected a health problem. "Autism?" he questioned.

"No!" I defended. "She wouldn't make eye contact if she had autism." *Besides*, I thought, *she has to be healthy. The medical reports said so.* I couldn't permit myself to think otherwise, despite the fact that Laura couldn't sit, roll over, coo, or eat like the other babies, even the younger ones, or like her paperwork reported she could.

Once we got home, reality set in. Laura didn't interact with toys. When we laid her on her tummy, she would either bang her head on the floor or lie still. She reacted the same way in her walker. She never tried to move it. She just banged her head. She never cared who held her, nor did she show a preference for Mommy or Daddy. Where was the happy, healthy girl we longed for? Why did everyone else get a walking, chatty child and we got a child who was banging her head on the floor? The stress weighed heavily on our marriage and family.

We started a barrage of appointments with physical, occupational, and speech therapists, special education teachers, neurologists, and ophthalmologists. They ordered everything from MRIs and CT scans to blood work. Soon the health department called regarding her high lead levels. And before long, Laura's veins formed scar tissue from all of the poking, making it harder to draw blood. Without a birth history, we didn't have much to go on. Doctors disagreed about her diagnosis. Some therapists projected rapid progress, while others wondered why progress wasn't being made. Our quiet Laura responded with full-blown screams.

So where was God in all of this? He was there amidst our anger, frustration, and denial. We were new Christians who were too busy trying to fix our daughter to call out to our Lord for help. God tried to assure me that He was in control, that I could stop being angry at the officials because He, not China, had placed Laura into our family, and that I could stop trying to fix Laura because He knew what was best and would not give us more than we could handle as a family. Through it all, our faith was strengthened beyond my imagination.

At age four, Laura is developmentally like a one-year-old. She doesn't speak, walk, or do much else without assistance. Unless God performs a miracle, she will be our little princess at home forever. But I'm thrilled to watch each and every tiny milestone, like feeding herself a Cheerios®, crawling a few inches, standing in her crib, reciprocating a smile, or laying her head on my shoulder.

God helped me to see that His ways are greater than mine. I had everything organized and planned perfectly. I wanted a healthy little girl, and I would give anything for Laura to be so healthy. But God gave me much more—the chance to be mom to a very special girl.

Laura's doctor and therapy appointments provide opportunities to share God's love, even if it's only through lending an ear to listen or giving a smile that says, "I know what you're going through, as only we moms of special kids truly understand."

Laura's challenges help those around us become more compassionate and patient towards those who are less able. God is teaching our sons that it's OK to be different, that we are all God's children no matter our appearance or capabilities.

Most importantly, God has opened my eyes to see that He provides what I need each day, not necessarily what I want. If I worry about tomorrow, or where Laura will be in twenty years, I will drive myself crazy. God never will leave us or forsake us. I can turn my cares over to Him so that my shoulders are much lighter.

One day, Laura will see God face-to-face. He will open His arms, welcome her home, and give her a beautiful voice for singing and a graceful body for dancing. Until then, He has handed her care over to us, and I'm thankful to Him for this beautiful life.

—Angie Miller

Prayer Points

When You built our family, Lord Jesus, You knew the challenges our child would face in our care. We thank You for his/her strengths, and we lift up his/her weaknesses. Give us sensitive hearts and resourceful minds to provide the best care and environment for him/her and our family. Strengthen each of us during evaluations, meetings, treatments, and in home and

Mom Mom and Pop Pop Cervone
congratulating our preschool graduate

school situations. Provide the people and assistance needed to ensure growth and development for our child.

Explanations

I hear a lot of adopted kids talk about feeling that something is missing in life, about not being wanted. I say, "Do you understand the lengths parents go to adopt? It's so much harder to adopt. Adopted children are wanted more than anybody, loved more than anyone."
—Ryan Dobson, adopted son of James and Shirley Dobson[3]

We try to talk about Noah's adoption any chance we get because we want him to understand how we became a family. We say things like, "When we visited you in Russia…" or, "Your first train ride was in Russia…" so his beginnings become part of his everyday language.

I remember the first in-depth conversation we had about his birth mom. It was his birthday, when he turned four. I especially thanked God for his birth mom that day. I told him, "Remember, you weren't in my belly. You were in your Russian mommy's belly."

With wisdom unlike most four-year-olds, Noah replied, "Him must miss me." I fought back tears, saying, "She probably does miss you. That's why we're thankful she let us become your mommy and daddy."

We can encourage our children to explore their feelings about adoption with prompts, such as:

- One thing I think about my birth mother/birth father is…
- Something good about being adopted is…
- Something hard about being adopted is…
- On my birthday, I wonder…

- One thing I like about my family is...
- I am like/unlike my birth family because...
- I am like/unlike my adoptive family because...

I cannot heal my child's wounds, only God can... As a parent, I am to be a channel of God's love and grace, in His holiness and His mercy to my daughter. I am not to be the one to fix her. I am to leave my child to the Savior and then let Him be the one to do the work in her life.
—Barbara Rainey[4]

One Family's Story: Prayers of Healing

As an adoptive mama, as well as an adopted person myself, I celebrate adoption. As someone who endured the loss of my first parents, though, I also know that adoption, by definition, involves loss. Before we ever were chosen, we were abandoned or relinquished.

As parents, it can be tempting to smooth over our children's earliest losses. We may hesitate to bring up the more difficult pieces of their stories or gloss over the hard parts of their early history. Longing for them to know they are entirely precious and beloved, we are quick to remind them of our love for them and their worthiness as God's beloved children.

While these things we tell them are true, we fail our children when we don't make room for them to acknowledge and grieve about what they lost prior to being enfolded into their forever family. Like a wound that's been bandaged, those deep hurts—even the ones we can't see—heal best when exposed to the air and the light.

In the second chapter of Exodus, the cries of God's people reached God's ears. God saw their suffering. God noticed, and God cared. My heart leapt within me when I first read those words. Unconvinced in my deepest places that I was worth loving, I longed for someone to see, hear, know, and care about my hurts.

It sounds crazy, but after the Israelites' cries reached God's ears, He chose Moses as his holy instrument of redemption—a pretty far-fetched plan, even to Moses! God chose to make His power and presence known through a human being. Personally, I think it was brilliant.

Since my early childhood, I've known in my head and even in my heart that God loves me. However, my soul longed for a human face to reflect the sadness and pain I experienced. Although I'd been assured I was loved and chosen, I needed someone to acknowledge the hurt and loss I'd endured. Graciously, God, to reflect His own care and compassion, provided those human faces to me in adulthood through the body of Christ.

I am convinced God is in the unlikely business of using humans to represent His face of love. Specifically, God uses adoptive parents to reflect, for our children, God's own countenance. When we demonstrate to our children that we see, hear, know, and care about both their joys and their sorrows, we reflect the truth of God's great compassion for them.

The chosen pattern of God's redemption was hinted at when Moses functioned as God's agent of deliverance. God's big game plan came to fruition, of course, in the person of Jesus Christ. God's fathomless mercy was poured out upon humanity in the person who, in identifying with our humanity, also saw, heard, understood, and cared.

Today, through the Holy Spirit, we are the vessels God uses to re-present His face of love. We do this as we recognize our children's hurts, listen to their cries, and acknowledge their losses. We are meant to be the agents God uses to heal our children's hearts.

Prayer

*Father, give me Your eyes to recognize my child's loss
and pain with eyes that truly see.
Father, give me Your ears to listen to my child's heart
with ears that truly hear.
Father, give me Your countenance to reflect Your face
of compassion for my child.
Father, use my face, body, and voice to embody Your
true Word.*

—Margot Starbuck

One Family's Story: Honoring a Birth Mother

Our three-year-old daughter from Guatemala loves to
hear her adoption story at bedtime. So for Mother's Day, we
buy a special balloon for her birth mom, whom she's never
met. We stand on our deck, and before she lets go of the
balloon, she whispers something to her birth mom. Then
she sends the balloon up into the air. This is one way we
show gratitude for her birth mother's decision and sacrifice,
and our daughter seems to enjoy it.

—Linda Ferrell

Celebrations

We had to celebrate this happy day. For your brother
was dead and has come back to life! He was lost, but
now he is found!

—Luke 15:32 NLT

When a "lost" child finds a forever family and has the
chance to become alive again, it is cause for celebration.
Public or private, small-scale or large, the child's presence
in the family can be celebrated every day.

Grandma and Granddad Scott and Noah
celebrating his 2nd birthday

Lifebooks

One way to celebrate adoption at home is to create a lifebook, a scrapbook that honors the child's life story. You don't have to be a scrapbooker to create a meaningful lifebook.

A lifebook tells a child's story using words and photographs. You can include answers to questions like, "Where did I come from?" and, "How did I get here?" If you're a scrapbooker, then you probably are comfortable with your lifebook project. If not, please don't be intimidated! A simple lifebook can be created from an inkjet printer, a photo album, or a memory album. Here are some ways to add those special touches regardless of your skill or comfort level:

1. **Start at the beginning—even if there is a lack of information.**

   Your child's story began before he or she was introduced into your family. Be sure to honor your child's beginnings by including information about his or her life and history prior to your family. If you don't have much background, you can include news and current events from the day of his birth or his hometown. You also can add what you were doing at the time to prepare for his arrival. Just be sure that your child, and not your waiting or feelings, remains the focus of the lifebook.

2. **Keep it age-appropriate, honest, and confidential.**

   Children enjoy reviewing their stories. Why not create several lifebooks according to your child's age? For preschoolers, create a colorful, sturdy photo book in a smaller size that's perfect for little fingers. As your child grows into school-age, work on a second lifebook together. This becomes an opportunity to discuss additional details of your child's story and gives permission for him or her to share memories and feelings.

   Always speak honestly about what you do and do not know about your child's background and birth family, being sensitive to what your child can understand at his or her age. Also, remember that it's your child's story and should be kept confidential.

3. **Consult children's books on adoption for style and wording ideas.**

   There are several great children's books that address adoption. Find one or two that appeal to you, and approach your storytelling with similar sensitivity and concepts.

4. Include adoption poems and page headings.

The internet is loaded with adoption resources. Find that special sentiment and include it on the appropriate page.

5. Add special adoption-related touches.

Your local craft store will have a variety of decorative papers and stickers; but you also can seek out adoption-specific embellishments. Look for state or country stickers as well as items depicting the adoption process, Adoption Day, and your forever family. The website www.scrapandtell.com is one of my favorite spots to shop for these items.

6. Give your child opportunities to view the lifebook.

A lifebook is meant to be viewed and discussed. Store it in an accessible place. Introduce opportunities for your child to look through it, making yourself available for questions. Be sensitive to your child's needs and cues. Understand that there may be a million questions one week, followed by weeks when the lifebook sits on the shelf.

Calendars

Preserving memories does not have to be labor intensive or time consuming. Jot down milestones and memories, such as "Baby's First Steps" and "First Day of Middle School" on special keepsake calendars. Or using personal photos, create your own calendars through an online photo service or at your local copy center. I create a parents' and grandparents' calendar of family photos as a Christmas present each year. I include everything from holiday, vacation, and everyday photos to snapshots of school craft projects. The calendar is a fun way to reminisce throughout the year.

Culture

It's important to celebrate your child's culture, whether your child hails from Ethiopia or the East Coast (say, New Jersey). Explore foods, history, music, and traditions specific to your child's background. Visit online retailers or bookstores for toys, games, books, cookbooks, clothing, and household items that represent his or her heritage. If there is no heritage specific to your child's birth family, help him or her learn about your culture as a newer member of the family.

Noah with St. Basil's Cathedral –
LEGO® Store, Orlando, Florida

One Family's Story: Rejoicing Reflection

It was the merry month of May,
And who would have ever guessed
The miracle that was about to come,
And make our family extra blessed.
A little man as calm as could be,
Was snuggled in a bed.
We picked him up and held him close,
And kissed him on his head.
If it was God's will to be done,
We let Him lead the way.
And into our little world,
Josh would come to stay!
The heavenly gift of a little boy,
Was more than we could have dreamed.
And even more we learned the lesson.
Of you just have to BELIEVE!
With smiles a plenty he brightens each day,
He's loved more than you know.
With new adventures to see and learn,
He's really starting to grow!
He might be strong like Moses,
Who definitely was born to lead.
Or maybe smart like Solomon,
Only the future holds the key.
Whatever Josh chooses,
He'll know we're always at his side
To love, advise, teach, and pray,
And in God's love he resides.
Thank you for our miracle,
Who's brought us so much love.
We wish you health and happiness,
And blessings from angels up above!

—Jacqueline Coury

Epilogue

Our Forever Family[1]

October 2010

I T'S BEEN FIVE years since Noah became our son. And while the needs are different, the prayers continue. In many ways, God is still writing our adoption story.

One day we hope to return to Russia to reintroduce Noah to his birth country. At age six, he vaguely understands having been in "another mommy's belly" but does not have any thought about its ramifications. We expect, at some point, to field new questions about his birth mother and the circumstances that made him available for adoption.

People often ask if we would do it all again. My answer is, "Yes, I would do it again for Noah, but probably not again to adopt an additional child." With that being said, let me add that adoption brought unanticipated changes and depth to my life—a new career; a greater sense of community through neighbors, Noah's elementary school, and our new church; and advocacy causes like orphans, special needs, and wellness (especially for moms). I get to be "fearfully and wonderfully me" like never before because life did not go according to my plans (pregnancy) but His.

Noah is a joy and well worth every tear, frustration, and sacrifice. It's obvious he was meant to be our son. I hope he never gets tired of hearing how glad I am to be his mommy.

—Michele

Appendix A: Noah's Adoption Story

M Y MOMMY AND daddy weren't always a mommy and daddy. They waited for me. One day Mommy asked God to bring her a baby. He whispered to her heart that He had heard her prayer but that they would need to wait.

> Wait on the Lord; Be of good courage, And He shall strengthen your heart; Wait, I say, on the Lord!
> —Psalm 27:14 NKJV

After a little while, Mommy and Daddy went to a doctor for help. Nothing helped. Mommy and Daddy were sad. But they kept asking God for a baby. He gave them promises that they would be parents someday. They knew they could trust Him. They asked Grandma and Granddad and Mom Mom and Pop Pop for support. Everyone at church was praying for them, too.

Sing, O barren, you who have not borne! Break forth into
singing, and cry aloud, you who have not labored with
child! All your children shall be taught by the LORD, and
great shall be the peace of your children.
—Isaiah 54:1a, 13 NKJV

Then Mommy and Daddy went to Bethany Christian
Services to talk about adoption. Bethany helps boys and
girls all over the world find forever families. They said that
they would help Mommy and Daddy find me in Russia so
that I could have a family. Mommy and Daddy decided to
name me Noah.

God sets the solitary in families.
—Psalm 68:6a NKJV

I will bring your descendants from the east, And gather
you from the west.
—Isaiah 43:5 NKJV

When Lamech was 182 years old, a son was born. He
named him Noah, saying, This one shall bring us relief
and comfort from our work...
—Genesis 5:28–29

Mommy and Daddy did a lot of paperwork to send to
Russia. They got my room ready, and they waited some
more. Mommy would get sad sometimes. But Daddy was
always there to remind her that everything would be OK.
They both wanted me so much. They wanted the waiting
to be over, too.

Mommy asked God why it wasn't easy for them to
become parents. He whispered to Mommy's heart again.
This time He said, "Because you will tell them [everyone]
that it was Me [that gave you the gift of a child]." In her

mind's eye, Mommy could see me. She pictured Pastor Chris Swansen dedicating me to God in front of all of our friends and family. She pictured telling everyone what God had done to answer all of their prayers for us.

At the same time, the Russian government was going through changes that affected adoptions. The waiting became longer than anyone thought it would be.

> The Lord will fight for you, and you shall hold your peace and remain at rest.
> —Exodus 14:14

During that time, Uncle Mike and Aunt Amy Somerfield threw a surprise "Waiting Party" so that some of Mommy and Daddy's friends could encourage them.

> The Lord will give strength to His people; The Lord will bless His people with peace.
> —Psalm 29:11 NKJV

Mommy and Daddy kept praying and waiting. Soon they had waited so long that their paperwork in Russia was expiring. They would need to do everything again. They were tired. They asked God if they should give up.

> And Simon (Peter) answered, 'Master, we toiled all night [exhaustingly] and caught nothing [in our nets]. But on the ground of Your word, I will lower the nets [again].'
> —Luke 5:5

After many months and many tears, Mommy and Daddy finally got the call they had been waiting for: the invitation to come visit me in Russia! They were very excited. They started packing and planning their trip immediately. The flight was nine hours long. Then they took an overnight train to get to my orphanage. Still, they couldn't wait to meet me.

Then on July 13, 2005, Mommy and Daddy held me in their arms for the very first time. They describe it as pure joy. Instantly, all of the waiting and the tears became a distant memory. They finally had met me, their son.

> For this child I prayed, and the LORD has granted me my petition which I asked of Him.
> —1 Samuel 1:27 NKJV

Soon they needed to return to the United States to wait for a court date for my adoption in Russia. While it was hard to say "good-bye," Mommy and Daddy had a peace that it was only a temporary separation and that I was being well cared for.

Mommy and Daddy celebrated my first birthday with a special dinner, presents, and cake. They also had a toy delivered to me at the orphanage so that I could celebrate, too. The very next morning, they received the wonderful news that they would be returning to Russia for court in September.

After many delays with their flights, they arrived in my city just two hours before court (one day later than they had planned). Still, God had everything under control. My adoption was finalized on September 8, and we became a family, just as God had planned all along!

God gave me a beautiful adoption story. And there's an even greater adoption that Mommy and Daddy will be teaching me about—how we all can be adopted into God's family through Jesus Christ. You can never be too young or too old to understand and accept God's gift of eternal life in heaven and a new life filled with love, joy, hope, and peace on earth as a part of His family. That you will understand this and be adopted into God's family is Mommy and Daddy's prayer for you, and for me, too.

I am Noah, the child Mommy and Daddy longed and prayed for, and this is how God made us a family. Now it's Mommy and Daddy and me!

Appendix B:
When Adoption
Hurts

We have talked a lot, and you will hear all of us talk about
the process of grieving with hope. That's what has kept
us breathing, that's what's kept us alive, is that while we
are grieving this process, there is a hope that we have.
We are a family with a lot of questions. But that's what
faith is. It's living with the questions. That doesn't mean
you have the answers. That's exactly what faith is. I know
that I will dance with Maria again someday.
> —Steven Curtis Chapman on daughter
> Maria's death[1]

WE APPROACH OUR adoptions with the high-
est of hopes and the biggest of dreams. But for
reasons usually unknown to us, things can go
wrong. Countries close their programs, birth mothers decide
to parent, a child has greater needs than we can handle, and
we're left holding pieces of shattered dreams. The pain can
run so deep that we question if we'll ever get out of bed
again, let alone attempt another adoption. Moreover, we

might be so angry and hurt that we don't want to pray, even if we could find the words.

One Family's Story: From Heartbreak to Healing

We adopted our daughter Heather from Vietnam through the "Operation Baby Lift" program (OBL) in April of 1975. Sadly, she was very ill, and she died just weeks after she arrived home to us. Three days after Heather's death, on the evening of her funeral, the adoption agency phoned to ask if we'd like to adopt one of three babies still in the hospital. Our daughter Jennie became the final baby placed through OBL.

At times like these we can rely on the Holy Spirit to pray on our behalf. Romans 8:26–28 says:

> So too the [Holy] Spirit comes to our aid and bears us up in our weakness; for we do not know what prayer to offer nor how to offer it worthily as we ought, but the Spirit Himself goes to meet our supplication and pleads in our behalf with unspeakable yearnings and groanings too deep for utterance. And He Who searches the hearts of men knows what is in the mind of the [Holy] Spirit [what His intent is], because the Spirit intercedes and pleads [before God] in behalf of the saints according to and in harmony with God's will. We are assured and know that [God being a partner in their labor] all things work together and are [fitting into a plan] for good to and for those who love God and are called according to [His] design and purpose.
>
> —Lana Noone

Other verses to pray:

O my God, I trust, lean on, rely on, and am confident in You. Let me not be put to shame or [my hope in You] be disappointed; let not my enemies triumph over me. Yes, let none who trust and wait hopefully and look for You be put to shame or be disappointed. . .

—Psalm 25:2–3

The Lord will give [unyielding and impenetrable] strength to His people; the Lord will bless His people with peace.

—Psalm 29:11

For I know the thoughts and plans that I have for you, says the Lord, thoughts and plans for welfare and peace and not for evil, to give you hope in your final outcome.

—Jeremiah 29:11

Endnotes

Preface

1. FamilyLife Today. "Counting the Cost of Adoption," Discovering Adoption series, November 14, 2007, by FamilyLife Ministries.

Chapter 1

1. Van den Boom, Joris-Jan, Photographer. "*1 Year Ago: Kids at the Orphanage.*" Photograph. Delft, Netherlands: Buro de Peper, March 30, 2009. http://www.flickr.com/photos/jorisjan/4476528275/ (accessed October 2, 2010).
2. "Steven Curtis Chapman Trivia and Quotes." http://www.tv.com/steven-curtis-chapman/person/94227/trivia.html (accessed September 12, 2009).
3. FamilyLife Today. "Strategies for Parenting Your Adopted Child," Understanding and Parenting Your Adopted Child series, May 10, 2005, by FamilyLife Ministries.

4. Humphrey, Nicole. "Scrapbooking Your Adoption Experience." http://scrapbooking.families.com/blog/scrapbooking-your-adoption-experience (accessed August 23, 2009).
5. Lana Noone, e-mail message to author, October 13, 2009.

Chapter 2

1. "Pearl S. Buck Quotes and Quotations." http://famous-quotesandauthors.com/authors/pearl_s_buck_quotes.html (accessed October 3, 2010).
2. "In Loving Memory of Derek Loux" (Memorial Service Program). http://www.josiahfund.org/DerekLouxProgram.pdf (accessed October 3, 2010).

Chapter 3

1. Kingsbury, Karen. "The Call to Adopt: How a Best-Selling Christian Author Doubled Her Family." http://karenkingsbury.com/aboutKaren/adoption/ (accessed September 15, 2009).
2. "E.M. Bounds Quotes and Quotations." http://famous-quotesandauthors.com/authors/e_m_bounds_quotes.html (accessed October 3, 2010).

Chapter 6

1. Author Unknown, "Relax My Dear" poem. Matted print.
2. Author Unknown, "Before I Was A Mom" poem. http://dltk-holidays.com/mom/before_mom.htm (accessed October 3, 2010).
3. Pearl S. Buck. BrainyQuote.com, Xplore Inc, 2010. http://www.brainyquote.com/quotes/authors/p/pearl_s_buck_2.html (accessed October 3, 2010).

4. FamilyLife Today. "Strategies for Parenting Your Adopted Child," Understanding and Parenting Your Adopted Child series, May 10, 2005, by FamilyLife Ministries.

Chapter 7

1. FamilyLife Today. "Adopting Deborah," Understanding and Parenting Your Adopted Child series, May 9, 2005, by FamilyLife Ministries.
2. FamilyLife Today. "Counting the Cost of Adoption," Discovering Adoption series, November 14, 2007, by FamilyLife Ministries.
3. "Ryan Dobson to Share His Passion for Life and Adoption." http://harborhouse.org/banquet/sharingbanquet2003.htm (accessed September 15, 2009).
4. FamilyLife Today. "Adopting Deborah," Understanding and Parenting Your Adopted Child series, May 9, 2005, by FamilyLife Ministries.

Epilogue

1. Cressman, Eric, Photographer. "*Scott Family.*" Photograph. Honey Brook, Pennsylvania, USA: Eric Cressman Photography, June 5, 2010.

Appendix B

1. "Steven Curtis Chapman Trivia and Quotes." http://www.tv.com/steven-curtis-chapman/person/94227/trivia.html (accessed September 12, 2009).

Many Thanks

I WOULD LIKE TO thank the following individuals and their families for contributing their adoption experiences to this project.

Michelle Kemper Brownlow and family live in southeastern PA on a former dairy farm turned best subdivision on the planet. When she's not writing for MomSpace.com, MomLogic.com, or her own blog (michellekemperbrownlowwrites4kids.blogspot.com), she enjoys writing picture books and teen novels.

Carmela shares her adoption story in loving memory of her late husband, Richard.

Betty Ann Cervone is the proud grandmother of Noah Scott, one of the cutest kids to come out of Russia. She serves as the best non-paid babysitter, housekeeper, and personal assistant a daughter and author could hope for.

Jacquelyn Coury knows that with God all things are possible, as evidenced by the miracle of her son Josh's adoption.

Linda Ferrell is the mother of three biological children and one adopted child.

Jennifer Greenman lives in Pennsylvania with her family and serves as President of the Philadelphia Chapter of Families for Russian and Ukrainian Adoption.

Laurel Greer is a wife, mother, and the Director of Rwandan Relations at 4-more.org. She blogged about her adoption experience at milestomyles.blogspot.com. Her mother-in-law, *Bonnie Greer*, contributed her poem about Myles to this project.

Linda Hursh is a mother of two who lives in Pennsylvania. She enjoys spending time with her family in the great outdoors.

Melinda Izzo is a wife and mother who works in the education field.

Bethany Martin and her husband live in a suburb of Philadelphia with their three-year-old daughter, who was adopted from Russia. They enjoy swimming, hiking, and spending time together as a family.

Angela Miller has a heart for Jesus and for orphans. She blogs at beyondthehorizon-miller.blogspot.com.

Nanette loves her daughter beyond words. Adoption reinforced her family's desire to trust God and put Him first in all decisions.

Lana Noone is the author of *Global Mom: Notes From a Pioneer Adoptive Family* and the mother of children adopted from Vietnam (Operation Baby Lift—1975) and Korea (1979).

Karin Prunty is a freelance writer (jacobsjourneyhome. blogspot.com) and photographer. She and her husband have ten wonderful children adopted from the US, China, and Guatemala. They live outside of Boston, Massachusetts.

Jill Savage is the founder of Hearts at Home (hearts-at-home.org) and blogs at jillsavage.org. She and her husband have five children and make their home in Central Illinois.

David Michael Smith of Georgetown, Delaware, says he hears God but doesn't always listen. When he does, he writes stories like "China Doll" and gets to share one of his gifts with the world. He is happily married to Geri and the proud parent of Rebekah Joy and Matthew Robert. David can be reached at davidandgeri@hotmail.com.

Lisa Spradling is the proud birth mother of Allison. The two enjoy a close relationship after reuniting several years ago.

Margot Starbuck is the author of *The Girl in the Orange Dress: Searching for a Father Who Does Not Fail*, a spiritual memoir about her adoption and reunion. She lives in Durham, North Carolina, with her husband, Peter, and their three children, lent to them by birth and adoption. Check out what Margot's up to at MargotStarbuck.com.

Patti Stoudt is a happily-married mother of three who enjoys sign language, homeschooling, and crisis pregnancy work.

Karen Webb is a mother of nine. She lives in Pennsylvania and enjoys singing, scrapbooking, painting, cooking, and spending time with her husband and children.

Carlos Whittaker is the proud father of two daughters (biological) and one son (adopted from South Korea).

In addition, I want to thank you, the reader, for allowing me to be a part of praying through *your* adoption. May God richly bless you and your family!

Please visit www.michelecscott.com for a current list of adoption and family resources.

Michele Cervone Scott
P.O. Box 427
Honey Brook, Pennsylvania 19344
USA
mail@michelecscott.com

E-book and e-reader versions of
Praying Through Your Adoption also are available.

WinePressPublishing
Great Books, Defined.

To order additional copies of this book call:
1-877-421-READ (7323)
or please visit our website at
www.WinePressbooks.com

If you enjoyed this quality custom-published book,
drop by our website for more books and information.

www.winepresspublishing.com
"Your partner in custom publishing."

9 781606 150832